# SOCIALISM OR BARBARISM

# SOCIALISM OR BARBARISM

## From the "American Century"
to the Crossroads

### ISTVÁN MÉSZÁROS

Monthly Review Press
New York

A shorter version of the essay "Socialism or Barbarism" was presented in Athens on October 19, 1999, at a conference on prospects of twenty-first century developments organized by the Greek bimonthly magazine OYTOPIA, edited by E. I. Bitsakis and published in OYTOPIA no. 39, March-April 2000.

Library of Congress Cataloging-in-Publication Data
Mészáros, István, 1930-
    Socialism or barbarism: from the "American Century" to the crossroads / István Mészáros.
        p.cm.
    Includes bibliographical references and index.
    ISBN 1-58367-051-3 (cloth) — ISBN 1-58367-052-1 (paper)
    1. Capitalism. 2. Imperialism. 3. Socialism. 4. Postmodernism. I. Title


HB501 .M6225 2001
335—dc21                                        2001030886


Monthly Review Press
122 West 27th Street
New York, New York 10001


Manufactured in Canada
10  9  8  7  6  5  4  3  2  1

# CONTENTS

This study is dedicated to Harry Magdoff and Paul M. Sweezy, whose contribution in the last fifty years—in their books and as editors of *Monthly Review*—to our awareness of imperialism and monopolistic developments has been second to none.

# FOREWORD

We have just left the twentieth century, described by capital's most vocal apologists as "the American century." This view is voiced as if the October Revolution of 1917, or the Chinese and Cuban Revolutions and the colonial liberation struggles in the following decades had never taken place, not to mention the humiliating defeat directly suffered by the mighty United States in Vietnam. Indeed, the uncritical defenders of the established order confidently anticipate that not only the coming century but the whole of the next millennium is destined to conform to the unchallengeable rules of *Pax Americana*. Yet, no matter how much the relation of forces has been realigned in capital's favor in the last decade, the deep-seated causes beneath the major social earthquakes of the twentieth century mentioned above—to which one could add quite a few more, positive and negative alike, including two world wars—have not been resolved by subsequent developments. On the contrary, with every new phase of forced postponement the capital system's contradictions can only be aggravated, bringing with them ever greater danger for the very survival of humanity.

The insolubility of our social antagonisms, coupled with capital's uncontrollability, may well continue to generate for some time the atmosphere of triumphalism as well as the disorienting illusions of permanency, as they did in the recent past. But in due course the accumulating and destructively intensifying problems must be confronted. For if the next century is really going to be capital's triumphant "American century," there will be no more centuries for humans afterwards, let alone a full millennium. Saying this has nothing to do with "anti-Americanism." In 1992 I expressed my conviction that

> The future of socialism will be decided in the United States, however pessimistic this may sound. I try to hint at this in the last section of *The Power of Ideology* where I discuss the problem of universality.[1] Socialism either can assert itself universally and in such a way that it embraces all areas, including the most developed capitalist areas of the world, or it won't succeed.[2]

Given the present stage of development, with its gravely intertwined problems crying out for a lasting solution, only a universally viable approach can work. But despite its enforced "globalization," capital's incurably iniquitous system is *structurally incompatible* with *universality* in any meaningful sense of the term.

# PART I

## SOCIALISM OR BARBARISM: FROM THE "AMERICAN CENTURY" TO THE CROSSROADS

### 1. CAPITAL—THE LIVING CONTRADICTION

1.1

Whatever claims are made for the ongoing process of globalization, there can be no universality in the social world without *substantive equality*. Evidently, therefore, the capital system, in all of its historically known or conceivable forms, is totally inimical even to its own—stunted and crippled—projections of globalizing universality. And it is immeasurably more inimical to the only meaningful realization of socially viable universality which would fully harmonize the universal development of the productive forces with the all-round development of the abilities and potentialities of the freely associated social individuals, because it would be based on their consciously pursued aspirations. In place of this the *potentiality* of capital's universalizing tendency is turned into the *actuality of dehumanizing alienation and reification*. To say it with Marx:

> When the limited bourgeois form is stripped away, what is wealth other than the universality of individual needs, capacities, pleasures, productive forces, etc., created through universal exchange? The full development of human mastery over the forces of nature, those of so-called nature as well as of humanity's own nature? The absolute working out of his creative potentialities, with no presupposition other than the previous historic development, which

makes this totality of development, i.e. the development of all human powers as such the end in itself, not as measured on a predetermined yardstick? When he does not reproduce himself in one specificity, but produces his totality? Strives not to remain something he has become, but is in the absolute movement of becoming? In bourgeois economics—and in the epoch of production to which it corresponds—this complete working out of the human content appears as a complete emptying-out, this universal objectification as total alienation, and the tearing-down of all limited, one-sided aims as sacrifice of the human end-in-itself to an entirely external end.[3]

The development of the—in principle universally applicable—functional division of labor constitutes the potentially liberating horizontal dimension of capital's labor process. However, this dimension is inseparable from the vertical or hierarchical division of labor within the framework of capital's command structure. The function of the vertical dimension is to safeguard the vital interests of the system by securing the continued expansion of surplus labor on the basis of the maximum practicable exploitation of the totality of labor. Accordingly, the horizontal structuring force is allowed to advance at any given time only to the extent to which it is firmly controllable in capital's reproductive horizon by the vertical dimension.

This means that it can follow its own dynamic only to the extent to which the ensuing productive developments remain containable within the parameters of capital's imperatives (and corresponding limitations). Capital's demand for vertical ordering always constitutes the overriding moment in the relationship between the two dimensions. But whereas in the ascending phase of the system's development the horizontal and vertical dimensions complement one another through their relatively flexible reciprocal interchanges, once the ascending phase is left behind the formerly overriding moment of a dialectical complex is turned into an ultimately *disruptive one-sided determination.* This brings with it grave limitations to productive development, together with a major crisis of accumulation fully in evidence in our own time. This is why the once promised potential universality in the development of the productive forces must be aborted, in the interest of safeguarding capital's self-oriented partiality and insurmountable structural hierarchy.

The capital system is articulated as a jungle-like network of contradictions that can only be more or less successfully *managed* for some time but never definitively *overcome.* At the roots of all of them we find the irreconcilable antagonism between capital and labor, always necessarily assuming the form of the *structural/hierarchical subordination of labour to capital,* no matter how elaborate and mystifying the attempts aimed at camouflaging this structural subordination. To name only some of the principal contradictions, we are confronted by those between:

~ production and its control

~ production and consumption;

~ production and circulation;

~ competition and monopoly;

~ development and underdevelopment (i.e. the "north-south" divide, both globally and within every particular country);

~ expansion pregnant with the seeds of crisis-producing contraction;

~ production and destruction (the latter often glorified as "productive" or "creative destruction");

~ capital's structural domination of labor and its insurmountable dependence on living labor;

~ the production of free time (surplus labor) and its crippling negation through the imperative to reproduce and exploit necessary labor;

~ authoritarian decisionmaking in the productive enterprises and the need for their "consensual" implementation;

~ the expansion of employment and the generation of unemployment;

~ the drive for economizing with material and human resources wedded to the most absurd wastefulness of these resources;

~ growth of output at all costs and the concomitant environmental destruction;

~ the globalizing tendency of transnational enterprises and the necessary constraints exercised by the national states against their rivals;

~ control over the particular productive units and the failure to control their comprehensive setting (hence the extremely problematical character of all attempts at planning in all conceivable forms of the capital system); and

~ the contradiction between the economically and the politically regulated extraction of surplus labor.

It is quite inconceivable to overcome even a single one of these contradictions, let alone their inextricably combined network, without instituting a radical alternative to capital's mode of social metabolic control[4]—an alternative based on *substantive equality* whose total absence is the common denominator and vitiating core of all social relations under the existing system.

What is also important to stress here is that—due to the structural crisis of the capital system as such, in contrast to the periodic conjunctural crises of capitalism witnessed in the past—the problems are fatefully aggravated at the present stage of development, putting on the historical agenda the need for a viable *overall control* of humanity's material productive and cultural interchanges as a matter of great urgency. Marx could still talk about the development of the capital system as one that, despite its own barriers and limitations, "enlarges the circle of consumption" and "tears down all the barriers which hem in the development of the forces of production, the expansion of needs, the all-sided development of production, and the exploitation and exchange of natural and mental forces."[5] In this spirit he could characterize the full unfolding of the capital system as "the *presupposition* of a new mode of production."[6] Today, there can be no question of *"all-sided development of production"* linked to the expansion of *human needs*. Thus, given the way in which capital's stunted globalizing tendency has actualized—and continues to enforce—itself, it would be quite *suicidal* to envisage capital's destructive reality as the presupposition of the much needed new mode of reproducing the sustainable conditions of human existence. As things stand today, capital's concern cannot be the "enlargement of the consumption circle," to the benefit of the "rich social individual" Marx talked about, but only its own enlarged reproduction at whatever cost. And the latter can be secured, at least for the time being, only by various modalities of destruction.

From the perverse standpoint of capital's "realization process," then, *consumption and destruction are functional equivalents*. Once upon a time the enlargement of the consumption circle could go hand in hand with the overriding imperative of capital's enlarged self-realization. With the end of capital's historical ascendancy the conditions of the system's expanded reproduction have been radically and irretrievably altered, pushing into the foreground overwhelmingly the destructive tendencies and, as their natural companion, catastrophic wastefulness. Nothing illustrates this better than the *"military-industrial complex"* and its continued expansion despite the pretenses of the "new world order" and its so-called "peace dividend" after the "end of the cold war." (We return to this complex of problems in Section 2.7.)

1.2

In line with these developments moreover the question of unemployment has been significantly altered for the worse. It is no longer confined to the "reserve army" waiting to be activated and brought into the framework of capital's productive expansion, as it used to be the case in the system's ascending phase, at times even to a prodigious extent. Now the grave reality of dehumanizing unemployment has assumed a chronic character, acknowledged even by the most uncritical defenders of capital—to be sure, in a self-justifying way, as if it had nothing whatever to do with the perverse nature of their cherished system—as "structural unemployment."

By contrast, in the postwar decades of undisturbed expansion the problem of unemployment was presumed to be permanently resolved. Thus one of the worst apologists of capital—Walt Rostow: a leading figure in President Kennedy's "brains trust"—arrogantly declared in a vacuous but everywhere massively promoted book that:

> There is every reason to believe, looking at the sensitivity of the political process to even small pockets of unemployment in modern democratic societies, that the sluggish and timid policies of the 1920s and 1930s with respect to the level of unemployment will no longer be tolerated in Western societies. And now the technical tricks of the trade—due to the Keynesian revolution—are widely understood. It should not be forgotten that Keynes set himself the task of defeating Marx's prognosis about the course of unemployment under capitalism; and he largely succeeded.[7]

In the same spirit Rostow and the whole army of bourgeois economists confidently predicted not only that the "pockets of unemployment in Western democracies" would be soon and forever turned into an oasis of "affluence" and prosperity, but that thanks to their recipes and "trade-tricks" of universally applicable "*modernization*" the Third World would also reach the same level of "development" and happy fulfilment as our "Western democracies." It was supposed to be in the preordained nature of the timeless universe that underdevelopment would be followed by capitalist "*take-off*," which in its turn inexorably brings with it a natural "*drive to maturity*," provided that the political forces of "Western democracies" prevent the evil deeds of trouble-making revolutionaries who are bent on interfering with this natural order.

This euphoria produced a generously financed industry of development studies, which produced much activity but few concrete results. With the onset of capital's structural crisis, neoliberal monetarism took over the ideological orienting positions up until then occupied by the high priests of Keynesian salvation. This removed the basic premise that had justified the expansion of the discipline. And when in the end it had to be admitted that the Keynesian "tricks of the trade" could never again regenerate the earlier "miracles" (that is, conditions described as "miracles" by those who at the time foolishly believed in them, not by their critical adversaries), the former propagandists of the Keynesian final solution of capital's defects simply turned their coats and, without the slightest murmur of self-criticism, invited all those who had not yet reached their own level of new transcendental enlightenment to wake up from their slumber and give their erstwhile hero a decent funeral.[8]

In this way the ideology of Third World modernization had to be—somewhat humiliatingly—abandoned. The issue was further complicated by the growing danger of ecological disaster. It became obvious that if the catastrophic levels of wastefulness and pollution produced by the model country of "modernization," the United States, were allowed to prevail even just in China and India, that would bring devastating consequences also to the idealized "Western democracies." Besides, the self-serving solution newly advocated by the United States—to buy "pollution rights" from Third World countries—is not only self-destructive, but also assumes the permanence of Third World underdevelopment.

Thus from now on everywhere, including the "Western democracies," the ideology of modernization had to be used as a new type of weapon, so as to clobber and disqualify "Old Labour" for refusing to be modernized by "New Labour"; that is, for failing to abandon, as "New Labour" has, even its mildly social-democratic principles and commitments. The new universally commended objectives were *"democracy and development"*: democracy as modelled on the US political consensus between the Republicans and the Democrats, as a result of which the working class is unceremoniously and completely *disenfranchised* even in a limited parliamentary sense; and development meaning nothing more than what can be readily squeezed into the empty shell of the most tendentious definition of formal democracy, to be imposed all over the world, from the "newly emergent democracies" of Eastern Europe and the former Soviet Union to Southeast Asia and Africa as well as to Latin America. As a leading propaganda organ of the US–dominated G7, the London *Economist* had put it with its inimitable cynicism:

> There is no alternative to the free market as the way to organize economic life. The spread of free market economics should gradually lead to multi-party democracy, because people who have free economic choice tend to insist on having free political choice too.[9]

For labor as the antagonist of capital, "free economic choice" in employment can only amount to submission to the orders emanating from the system's expansionary imperatives; and for ever-increasing numbers of those not so "lucky," it means the exposure to the indignities and the extreme hardship caused by chronic structural unemployment. The "free political choice" that can be exercised within the framework of "multiparty democracy" boils down in reality to the bitterly resigned acceptance of the consequences of an ever-narrowing political *consensus*, which made no less than 77 percent of British voters—and almost the same percentage of people also in some other countries of the European Community—refuse to participate in such a meaningless ritual at the last nationwide election, when they were called upon to choose their members of the European parliament.

In much the same way as in the economic field, we have witnessed dramatic reversals in the field of political representation and management as well, as a result of capital's narrowing margins. In the domain of production the ascending phase of capital's development had brought with it a massive expansion of employment, leaving its place in our time to the dangerous trend of chronic unemployment. As to the political domain, we could see a move from the dramatic enlargement of the franchise, to the point of universal franchise and the corresponding formation of labor's mass parties, leading to a major reversal in the not formal but effective and complete disenfranchising of labor in its parliamentary political setting. It is enough to think in this respect of political formations like New Labour and its equivalents on the "other side," operating the most peculiar form of "democratic decision making" in tiny kitchen cabinets, and ruthlessly imposing the wisdom of "there is no alternative" on any dissenting voice, even if it happens to surface by some accident in the rubber-stamping national cabinets.

### 1.3

The devastating trend of chronic unemployment now affects even the most advanced capitalist countries. At the same time, the people still in employment in those countries have to endure a worsening of their material conditions of existence, admitted even by the official statistics. For the end of capital's historical ascendancy also brought with it a *downward equalization of the differential rate of exploitation.*[10]

The end of "Third World modernization" highlights a quite fundamental problem in the development of the capital system. It underlines the far-reaching historical significance of the fact that capital failed to complete its system as global capitalism, i.e. as the overwhelmingly economic regulation of the extraction of *surplus labor as surplus value*. Despite all past fantasies of "take-off" and "drive to maturity," today almost half of the world's population have to reproduce their conditions of existence in ways which stand in sharp contrast to the idealized "market mechanism" as the overwhelmingly dominant regulator of the social metabolism. Instead of completing itself as a properly capitalist global system, capital, apart from the countries where its economic mode of controlling the appropriation of surplus labor prevailed, also succeeded in creating *enclaves of capitalism*, with a more or less vast *non-capitalist hinterland*. India in this respect is an obvious example, China, by contrast, is a much more complicated one, in that its state cannot be qualified as capitalist. (Nevertheless, the country has some powerful capitalist enclaves, linked to a non-capitalist hinterland with well over one billion people.) This is in a way analogous to some past colonial empires, e.g. the British. Britain exercised an overall political-military control over India, fully exploiting its capitalist economic enclaves, leaving at the same time the overwhelming majority of the population to their own resources of pre-colonial and colonially aggravated hand-to-mouth existence.

Nor is it conceivable, for a variety of reasons—including the untenable and ungeneralizable structural articulation of "advanced capitalism," with its catastrophically wasteful decreasing rate of utilization as a major condition of its continued expansion—that this failure of capitalism will be remedied in the future. Thus the failure of capitalist modernization of the Third World, despite all the efforts invested in it in the postwar decades of expansion, draws our attention to a fundamental structural defect of the whole system.

One more problem must be briefly mentioned in this context: the hybridization in evidence even in the most advanced capitalist countries. Its principal dimension is the ever-greater direct and indirect involvement of the state in safeguarding the continued viability of capital's mode of social metabolic reproduction. Despite all protestations to the contrary, coupled with neo-liberal fantasies about "rolling back the boundaries of the state," the capital system could not survive for a week without the massive backing it constantly receives from the state. I have discussed this problem elsewhere, and therefore a brief mention should suffice here. What Marx called the "extraneous help" given by Henry VIII and others to early capitalist development has reappeared in the twentieth century in an unimaginably massive form, from "common agricultural policies" and export guarantees to immense state-financed research funds and the insatiable appetite of the military industrial complex.[11] What makes the problem much worse is that no amount of this extraneous help is ever enough. Capital, at the present phase of historical development, has become totally dependent on an ever-increasing provision of it. In this respect, too, we are approaching a systemic limit in that we are confronted by the chronic insufficiency of extraneous help in regard to what the state is now capable of delivering. Indeed, the structural crisis of capital is inseparable from the chronic insufficiency of such extraneous help under conditions in which the defects and failures of this antagonistic system of societal reproduction call for an unlimited supply of it.

## 2. THE POTENTIALLY DEADLIEST PHASE
## OF IMPERIALISM

### 2.1

One of the weightiest contradictions and limitations of the system concerns the relationship between the globalizing tendency of transnational capital in the economic domain and the continued dominance of the national states as the comprehensive political command structure of the established order. The efforts of the dominant powers to make their own national states triumph over the others and thereby prevail as the state of the capital system as such have precipitated humankind into the bloodletting vicissitudes of two horrendous world wars in the twentieth century. Nonetheless, the national state remained the ultimate arbiter of comprehensive socioeconomic and political decision making as well as the real guarantor of the risks undertaken by all significant transnational economic ventures. Obviously, this is a contradiction of such magnitude that it cannot be assumed indefinitely to endure, whatever the endlessly repeated rhetoric pretending to resolve this contradiction through the discourse on "democracy and development" and its tempting corollary: "Think global, act local." This is why the question of imperialism must be brought to the forefront of critical attention.

Many years ago Paul Baran rightly characterized the radical change in the postwar international power relationships in the capitalist world and "the growing inability of the old imperialist nations to hold their own in face of the American quest for expanded influence and power," insisting that "the assertion of American supremacy in the 'free' world implies the reduction of Britain and France (not to speak of Belgium, Holland and Portugal) to the status of junior partners of American imperialism."[12] He also quoted the sobering words of the London *Economist*, pleading with characteristic subservience that "We must learn that we are not the Americans' equals now, and cannot be. We have a right to state our minimum national interests and expect the Americans to respect them. But this done, we must look for their lead."[13] A similar plea for the acceptance of American leadership—but perhaps not yet fully resigned to handing over to the United States, in some form or other, the British Empire—was expressed a quarter of a century earlier by the London *Observer*, saying with enthusiasm about President Roosevelt that "America has found a man. In him the world must find a leader."[14]

And yet, the end of the British Empire—together with all the others—was already foreshadowed in Roosevelt's first inaugural address, which made it absolutely clear that as president of the United States he "shall spare no effort to *restore world trade by international economic readjustment*."[15] And, in the same spirit, a few years later he advocated the right "to trade in an atmosphere of freedom *from unfair competition and domination by monopolies at home or abroad*."[16] Thus, the writing was on the wall for the British Empire from the beginning of Roosevelt's presidency. The question of colonialism made Roosevelt's relationship with Churchill a very unhappy one for the latter. This was revealed in a press briefing—partially off the record—which Roosevelt gave on his return from the Yalta Conference with Churchill and Stalin. Concerning the question of

French Indochina, Roosevelt proposed a transitional trusteeship before independence as the solution, so as to:

> educate them for self-government. It took fifty years for us to do it in the Philippines. Stalin liked the idea. China [Chiang Kai-Shek] liked the idea. The British don't like it. It might bust up their empire, because if the Indochinese work together and eventually get their independence, the Burmese might do the same thing to England.
>
> QUESTION: Is that Churchill's idea on all territory out there, he wants them all back, just the way they were?
>
> PRESIDENT: Yes, he is mid-Victorian on all things like that.
>
> QUESTION: This idea of Churchill's seems inconsistent with the policy of self-determination?
>
> PRESIDENT: Yes, that is true.
>
> QUESTION: Do you remember the speech the Prime Minister made about the fact that he was not made Prime Minister of Great Britain to see the Empire fall apart?
>
> PRESIDENT: Dear old Winston will never learn on that point. He has made his specialty on that point. This, of course, is off the record.[17]

Naturally, in the "international economic readjustment" he advocated—a readjustment arising in the first place from the 1929–1933 great world crisis and rendered ever more imperative for America through the onset of another recession in the country just before the outbreak of the Second World War—the whole of the British Empire was at stake. For Roosevelt believed that "India should be granted commonwealth status during the war and the choice of complete freedom five or ten years afterwards. The most galling suggestion, to old-line Britishers, was his proposal at Yalta that Hong Kong (as well as Dairen) be made into an international free port. His entire position seemed, in fact, naïve and wrong-headed from the British point of view. They felt that he misrepresented the aims and results of royal imperialism. More important, they warned that breakup of the Empire would weaken the West in a world of "power politics." It would leave dangerous areas of confusion and strife—'power vacuum' into which potential aggressors (the Reds) could move."[18]

With the appearance of the incomparably more powerful imperialist competitor, the United States, the fate of the British Empire was sealed. This was made even more pressing and in the colonies deceptively appealing because Roosevelt could present his policies aimed at achieving American international supremacy with the rhetoric of freedom to all, and indeed even with a claim to universally acceptable "destiny." He did not hesitate to declare that "a better civilization than any we have known is in store for America and by our example, perhaps, for the world. Here destiny seems to have taken a long look."[19] In no time at all after deriding the transparently imperialist ideological justifications of "old-line Britishers," the propaganda slogans of the latter were fully adopted as their own by the Americans, justifying their military interventions in Indochina and elsewhere in the name of preventing the generation of a "power vacuum" and blocking the possibility of the "domino effect" (produced by "the Reds"). But this could only surprise those who continued to nourish illusions about the "end of imperialism."

## 2.2

To understand the seriousness of the present situation we have to put it in historical perspective. The early modern imperialist penetration of various parts of the globe was of a rather different kind when compared with the incomparably more extensive—as well as intensive—penetration of some leading capitalist powers into the rest of the world in the last few decades of the nineteenth century. The contrast was forcefully underlined by Harry Magdoff:

> The same type of thinking that approaches the concept of economic imperialism in the restricted balance-sheet sense usually

also confines the term to control (direct or indirect) by an industrial power over an underdeveloped country. Such a limitation ignores the essential feature of the new imperialism that arises in the late nineteenth century: the competitive struggle among the industrial nations for dominant positions with respect to the world market and raw material sources. The structural difference which distinguishes the new imperialism from the old is the replacement of an economy in which many firms compete by one in which a handful of giant corporations in each industry compete. Further, during this period, the advance of transportation and communication technology and the challenge to England by the newest industrial nations [like Germany] brought two additional features to the imperialist stage: the intensification of competitive struggle in the world arena and the maturation of a truly international capitalist system. Under these circumstances, the competition among groups of giant corporations and their governments takes place over the entire globe: in the markets of the advanced nations as well as in those of the semi-industrialized and non-industrialized nations.[20]

With the successful imposition of American hegemony in the postwar world with its roots in the period of Roosevelt's first presidency, as we have seen above—we have been subjected to a third phase in the development of imperialism, with the gravest possible implications for the future. For now the catastrophic dangers that would go with a global conflagration, as experienced in the past, are self-evident even to the most uncritical defenders of the system. At the same time, no one in their right mind could exclude the possibility of the eruption of a deadly conflict, and with that the destruction of humankind. Yet, nothing is really done in order to resolve the underlying massive contradictions that point in that fateful direction. On the contrary, the continued enhancement of the economic and military hegemony of the one remaining superpower—the United States of America—casts an ever-darkening shadow on the future.

We have reached a new historical stage in the transnational development of capital: one in which it is no longer possible to avoid facing up to a fundamental contradiction and structural limitation of the system. That limitation is its grave failure to constitute the state of the capital system as such, as complementary to its transnational aspirations and articulation, so as to overcome the explosive antagonisms between national states that have characterized the system in constantly aggravated form in the last two centuries.

Capitalist rhetoric even at its best, as successfully practiced by Roosevelt in a situation of emergency, can be no substitute in this respect. Roosevelt's rhetoric—nostalgically remembered by many intellectuals on the left in the United States even today—was relatively successful precisely because it was readily apparent that a situation of emergency existed.[21] Although it greatly overstated the universal validity of the advocated actions and even more heavily understated or quite simply misrepresented the empire-building American elements, there was nevertheless some communality of interests both in addressing the symptoms of the world economic depression (even if not their causes, which tended to be reduced to "bad morals" equated with "bad economics" and to the actions of "blindly selfish men"[22]) and in the US participation in defeating Hitler's Germany. Today, by contrast, instead of the best rhetoric of the "New Deal" years we are bombarded with the worst kind: a cynical camouflage of reality which presents the most blatant US imperialist interests as the universal panacea of *"multiparty democracy,"* the tendentiously selective advocacy of *"human rights."* This advocacy of human rights can happily accommodate, among many others, the Turkish genocide against the Kurds, or the extermination of half a million Chinese in Indonesia at the time of installing Suharto, and of hundreds of thousands of people in East Timor later on by the same US client regime. What was once denounced as "domination by monopolies at home and abroad" is now presented in this discourse as the "free market."

Today competition among groups of giant corporations and their governments has a major qualifier: the overwhelming power of the United States dangerously bent on assuming the role of the state of the capital system as such, subsuming under itself by all means at its disposal all rival powers. The fact that this objective cannot be successfully accomplished on a lasting basis represents no deterrent to the forces ruthlessly pushing for its realization. And the problem is not simply some subjective misconception. As with every major contradiction of the given system, objective conditions make it imperative to pursue now the strategy of hegemonic domination by one economic and military superpower, at whatever cost, in order to try to overcome the structural cleavage between transnational capital and national states. However, the very nature of the underlying contradiction foreshadows the necessary failure of this strategy in the longer run. There have been many attempts to address the issue of potential conflagrations and the way of remedying them, from Kant's dream of perpetual peace overseen by a future League of Nations to the institutional establishment of such a league after the First World War, and from the solemnly declared principles of the Atlantic Charter to making operational the United Nations organization. They all proved to be woefully inadequate to the envisaged task. And no wonder. For the failure of instituting a "world government" on the basis of the established mode of social metabolic reproduction arises from the fact that here we are facing one of the absolute, untranscendable limits of the capital system itself. It goes without saying that the failure of labor's structural antagonist is very far from being a cause for comfort.

2.3

Imperialist domination is, of course, nothing new in American history, even if it has been justified—in President Roosevelt's words—as "fifty years of educating the Filipino people for self-government" (not to forget well over fifty years of "further education" through the agency of US proxies like Marcos and his successors). As Daniel B. Schirmer emphasized in his penetrating and meticulously documented book on the short-lived anti-imperialist movement in the United States at the turn of the century:

> The Vietnam War is only the last, most prolonged and most brutal of a series of United States interventions in the affairs of other peoples. The invasion of Cuba sponsored by United States authorities failed at the Bay of Pigs, but intervention has been more effective on other occasions, as in the Dominican Republic, Guatemala, British Guiana, Iran and the Congo. Nor is the list complete; other colonial peoples (and some European as well) have felt the effects of aggressive American intrusion upon their domestic policies, whether or not in the form of outright violence. . . . Present-day policies of counter-insurgency and intervention have their source in events that occurred at the opening of the twentieth century. Then the United States defeated Spain in war and stripped her of colonies in the Caribbean and the Pacific, taking Puerto Rico outright, giving Cuba nominal independence, and annexing the Philippines after first suppressing a nationalist revolution in those islands by force. What particularly distinguishes modern foreign policy from the Mexican war and the Indian wars for most of their span is that it is the product of another era in American history and comes in response to decisively different social pressures. Modern foreign policy is associated with the rise of the large-scale corporation, industrial and financial, as the dominant economic force in the country, exerting a most powerful influence upon the government of the United States. The Spanish-American war and the war to subdue Aguinaldo and the Philippine insurgents were the first foreign wars conducted as a consequence of this influence, the first wars of modern corporate America.[23]

When President Roosevelt proclaimed the strategy of "international economic readjustments" in his first inaugural address, his move indicated a determination to work for the dissolution of all colonial empires, not only the British. Like other major historical departures, this approach had its predecessor several decades earlier. In fact it was closely connected with the "open door policy" declared at the turn of the century.

The so-called open door that was demanded from other countries envisaged economic penetration (in contrast to direct colonial military occupation), keeping characteristically quiet about the overwhelming political domination that went with it. No wonder, therefore, that many people called the "open door policy" utterly hypocritical. When in 1899, in the name of such policy, the US declined to establish a colonial enclave in China, alongside the others as their equal, this was not due to liberal enlightenment or to democratic compassion. The opportunity was turned down because—as the most dynamic articulation of capital by that time—the United States wanted the whole of China, in due course, for itself. Such design became absolutely clear in the course of subsequent historical developments, reaching down all the way into our own time.

However, accomplishing world domination through the open door policy—given the relation of forces in the overall configuration of the major imperialist powers—was hopelessly premature at the turn of the century. The frightful bloodletting of the First World War was needed, as well as the unfolding of the grave world economic crisis after the short-lived period of reconstruction, before the Rooseveltian version of the strategy could be announced. Moreover, it needed an even greater bloodletting in the Second World War, coupled with the emergence of the United States in the course of that war as by far the greatest economic power, before the implementation of the Rooseveltian strategy could be forcefully attempted. This was done toward the end and in the immediate aftermath of the Second World War. The only remaining major complication—the existence of the Soviet system (since the additional complicating factor of China materialized with finality only in 1949)—was considered strictly temporary. This view was confidently asserted in the numerous declarations of Secretary of State John Foster Dulles concerning the policy of "rolling back communism."

Thus, in the course of twentieth-century developments we have reached a point where the competitive coexistence of imperialist powers can no longer be tolerated, no matter how much lip service is paid to the so-called polycentric world. As Baran rightly argued even in 1957, the proud owners of former colonial empires had been cut down in size to play the role of "junior partners of American imperialism." When the future of imperial possessions was discussed toward the end of the war, British concerns were swept aside as the hopelessly "mid-Victorian" notions of "dear old Winston." De Gaulle was not even consulted.[24] The Belgian, the Dutch and the Portuguese did not even enter the picture. All talk about the "polycentric world" under the principle of some sort of inter-state equality belongs to the realm of pure fantasy, if not to that of cynical ideological camouflage. Of course, there is nothing surprising about that. For "pluralism" in the world of capital can only mean the *plurality of capitals* and within such a plurality there can be no consideration of equality. On the contrary, it is always characterized by the most iniquitous pecking order of structural hierarchies and corresponding power relations, favoring always the stronger in their quest to gobble up the weaker. Thus, given the inexorability of capital's logic, it was only a question of time before the unfolding dynamism of the system had to reach the stage also at the level of inter-state relations when one hegemonic superpower had to overrule all of the less powerful ones, no matter how big, and assert its—ultimately unsustainable and for humanity as a whole most perilous—exclusive claim to being the state of the capital system as such.

2.4

Most significant in this respect is the attitude assumed in relation to the question of *national interests*. On the one hand, their legitimacy is forcefully asserted when the issues at stake affect, directly or indirectly, the presumed interests of the United States, not hesitating to use even the most extreme forms of military violence, or the threat of such violence, to impose their arbitrary decisions on the rest of the world. On the other hand, however, legitimate national interests of other countries are arrogantly dismissed as intolerable "nationalism'" and even as "ethnic pandaemonium."[25] At the same time, the United Nations and other international organizations are treated as playthings of the United States, and defied with utmost cynicism when their resolutions are not palatable to the guardians of the more or less openly declared US national interests. Examples are countless. About some recent ones Chomsky sharply commented: "The highest authorities explained with brutal clarity that the World Court, the UN, and other agencies had become irrelevant because they no longer follow US orders, as they did in early postwar years. . . . [U]nder Clinton the defiance of world order has become so extreme as to be of concern even to hawkish policy analysts."[26]

To add insult to injury, the United States refuses to pay its huge debt of United Nations membership arrears, while imposing its policies on the organization, including the cuts of funds for the chronically underfunded World Health Organization. This blatant obstructionism was noted even by such establishment figures as Jeffrey Sachs whose devotion to the cause of a US-dominated "market economy" is beyond doubt. He wrote in a recent article: "The failure of the United States to pay its UN dues is surely the world's most significant default on international obligations. . . . America has systematically squeezed the budgets of UN agencies, including such vital ones as the World Health Organization."[27]

It is necessary to mention here also the efforts—both ideologi-cal and organizational—invested in bypassing the national frame-work of decisionmaking. The superficially tempting slogan "Think global, act local" is an interesting case in point. For obviously the people in general, who are deprived of all meaningful power of decision-making on a broader scale (other than the abdicating electoral ritual), might find it just feasible to intervene in some way at the strictly local level. Moreover, no one could deny the potential importance of appropriate local action. However, the "global" to which we are expected to pay uncritical attention—meekly subscribing to the theses about the powerlessness of national governments and the inevitability of multinational glo-balization, which tendentiously misdescribe the *national transnational corporations* (heavily dominated by the United States) as "multina-tional" and thereby universally acceptable—is totally vacuous without its complex relations to the particular national communi-ties. Besides, once the "global" is divorced from its manifold national settings, diverting attention from the intertwined contra-dictory interstate relations, the call to act "locally" becomes utterly myopic and ultimately meaningless.[28] If democracy is thus con-fined to such decapitated "local action," then the "global decision making and action" that inevitably affects the life of every single individual can be exercised in the most authoritarian fashion by the dominant economic and political forces—and of course pre-dominantly the United States—in accord with the position occu-pied by them in the global pecking order of capital. The funds invested by the World Bank and other US-dominated organizations in trying to enhance the "local" at the expense of the national, attempting to enlist the support of academic and other intellectual elites through well-sponsored conferences and research projects (especially but not exclusively in the Third World), indicate a design to create a "world government" that effectively sidesteps the potentially most troublesome decisionmaking processes of the intermediary national level, with its unavoidable recalcitrance, and to legitimate the blatantly authoritarian domination of social life by a "world government" ruthlessly imposed from above in the name of the fictitious democracy synonymous with the pretended "local action" of "regular rubbish collections."

### 2.5

The manifestations of US economic imperialism are too numerous to be listed here. I have discussed some of the salient issues in the past, including issues which have aroused protests even from conservative politicians—against "technology transfer regulations, American protection laws, extraterritorial controls coordinated through the Pentagon and protected by Congress,"[29] and "funds channeled into the largest and richest companies on earth [in such a way that if the ongoing process continues] unchecked it will buy its way through sector after sector of the world's advanced technologies."[30] I have also discussed in the same article industrial advantage from military secrecy, direct trade pressures applied by the US legislative and executive branches of government, and the real debt problem in the world: that is, the astronomical debt of the United States itself, imposed by the dominant imperialist power on the rest of the world, for as long as the latter can continue to pay for it.[31]

Protests against "dollar imperialism" are often voiced, but to no avail. The economic imperialism of the country remains secure for as long as the United States retains its overwhelmingly dominant position not only through the dollar as the privileged world economic currency, but also in ruling all of the international organs of economic interchange, from the IMF to the World Bank and from GATT to its successor, the World Trade Organization. Today in France many people protest against "American economic imperialism" on account of the punitive tariffs recently imposed on

them by the United States under the pretended independent judg-
ment of the WTO. The same kind of measures were unceremoniously
imposed on Japan several times in the past, ending as a rule with the
reluctant or willing submission by the Japanese authorities to the
American dictates. If in the last round of punitive tariffs imposed on
Europe Britain was treated somewhat more leniently, that was only
as a reward for the total servility of the current British "New Labour"
government toward all orders from Washington. But even so, skir-
mishes of an international trade war reveal a very serious trend, with
far-reaching potential consequences for the future.

Similarly, the prepotent intervention of US governmental agencies
in the field of high technology, both military and civil, cannot be
assumed to endure indefinitely. In a crucial area—computer technology, both hardware and software—the situation is extremely serious.
To mention only one case, Microsoft enjoys an almost completely
monopolistic position in the world, and its software monopoly
massively restricts the choice of suitable hardware. But well beyond
that, it was brought to light a short while ago that a secret code
embedded in Microsoft software enables the US security and military
services to spy on everybody in the world who uses Microsoft
Windows and the Internet.

In another, literally vital, area—the production of genetically
modified foods by giant transnational corporations, like Monsanto—
the US government is doing everything it can to ram down the throats
of the rest of the world the products whose adoption will compel
agriculturalists everywhere to buy again and again the non-renewable
seeds from Monsanto and thus secure absolute domination for the
United States in the field of agriculture. The attempts to "patent genes"
for US corporations serve a similar purpose.

US attempts to impose "intellectual property rights"[32] on the
rest of the world through the agency of the WTO—aimed, among
other things (including vast economic interests), at securing the

permanent domination of world cinema and television by the third- and even tenth-rate Hollywood products with which we are constantly flooded—have generated cries of "US cultural imperialism." At the same time, the phenomenally well financed "business culture imperialism," in the form of pushing the penetration of the US army of "management consultancy" everywhere in the world, is part of the same picture.

But perhaps the most serious of the ongoing trends of economic and cultural domination is the rapacious and frightfully wasteful way the United States grabs to itself the world's energy and prime material resources: *25 percent of them for just 4 percent of the world's population*, with immense and relentlessly accumulating damage to the environmental conditions of human survival. And that is not all. For, in the same vein, the United States continues its active sabotage of all international efforts aimed at introducing some form of control in order to limit, and perhaps by 2012 to some degree reduce, the ongoing catastrophic trend of environmental damage, no longer deniable even by the worst apologists of the system.

### 2.6

The military dimension of all this must be taken very seriously. It is no exaggeration to say—in view of the formerly quite unimaginable destructive power of armaments accumulated in the second half of the twentieth century—that we have entered *the most dangerous phase of imperialism in all history*. For what is at stake today is not the control of a particular part of the planet—no matter how large—putting at a disadvantage but still tolerating the independent actions of some rivals, but the control of its totality by one hegemonic economic and military superpower, with all means—even the most extreme authoritarian and, if needed, violent military ones—at its disposal. This is what the ultimate rationality of globally developed capital requires, in its vain attempt to bring under control its irreconcilable antagonisms. The trouble is, though, that such rationality—which can be written without inverted commas, since it genuinely corresponds to the logic of capital at the present historical stage of global development—is at the same time the most extreme form of irrationality in history, including the Nazi conception of world domination, as far as the conditions required for the survival of humanity are concerned.

When Jonas Salk refused to patent his discovery, the polio vaccine, insisting that it would be like wanting "to patent the sun," he could not imagine that the time would come when capital would attempt to do just that, trying to patent not only the sun but also the air, even if that had to be coupled with dismissing any concern about the mortal dangers which such aspirations and actions carried with them for human survival. For the ultimate logic of capital in its processes of decision making can only be of a *categorically authoritarian* "top-down" variety, from the microcosms of small economic enterprises to the highest levels of political and military decisionmaking. But how can one *enforce* the patents taken out on the sun and the air?

There are two prohibitive obstacles in this regard, even if capital—in its drive to demolish its own untranscendable limits— must refuse to acknowledge them. The first is that the *plurality of capitals* cannot be eliminated, no matter how inexorable and brutal the monopolistic trend of development manifest in the system. And the second, that the corresponding *plurality of social labor* cannot be eliminated, so as to turn the total labor force of humankind, with all its national and sectional varieties and divisions, into the mindless "obedient servant" of the hegemonically dominant section of capital. For labor in its insurmountable plurality can never abdicate its right of access to the air and the sun; and even less can it survive for capital's continued benefit—an absolute must for this mode of controlling social metabolic reproduction—without the sun and the air.

Those who say that today imperialism does not involve the military occupation of territory not only underrate the dangers we face but also accept the most superficial and misleading appearances as the substantive defining characteristics of imperialism in our time, ignoring both history and the contemporary trends of development. For one thing, the US militarily occupies territory in no less than *sixty-nine countries* through its military bases: a number that continues to expand with the enlargement of NATO. Those bases are not there for the benefit of the people—the grotesque ideological justification—but for the benefit of the occupying power, so as to be able to dictate policies as it pleases.

In any case, the direct military occupation of colonial territories in the past could only be partial in extent. How could the small population of England otherwise have ruled the incomparably larger population and territories of its immense empire, above all India? Nor was such disproportionality an exclusive characteristic of the British Empire. As Renato Constantino reminded us in relation to the Philippines:

> From its inception, Spanish colonization operated more through religion than through force, thus profoundly affecting consciousness. This enabled the authorities to impose tributes, forced labor and conscription despite the small military force. Without the work of the priests, this would have been impossible. The priests became the pillars of the colonial establishment; so much so that it became a clerical boast that "in each friar in the Philippines the king had a captain general and a whole army." The molding of consciousness in the interest of colonial control was to be repeated on another plane by the Americans who after a decade of massive repression operated likewise through consciousness, this time using education and other cultural institutions.[33]

China, another vitally important example, was *never* militarily occupied, except for a small part of its territory. Not even when the Japanese invaded it with massive military forces. Yet, for a long time before that the country was completely dominated by foreign powers. So much so in fact that the young Mao sarcastically commented that "when the foreigner farts it must be hailed as heavenly perfume." What mattered in all imperialist ventures was always the ability to impose *dictates* on the dominated country on a *continuing basis*, using punitive military interventions only when the "normal" way of ruling was challenged. The famous expression *"gunboat diplomacy"* well encapsulated what was feasible and practicable with the available military resources.

The principal characteristics of such imperialist domination remain with us also today. The multiplication of the destructive power of the military arsenal available today—especially the catastrophic potential of aerial weapons—has to some extent modified the forms of imposing imperialist dictates on a country to be subdued, but not their substance. In all probability the ultimate form of threatening the adversary in the future—the new gunboat diplomacy—will be *nuclear blackmail*. But its objective would be analogous to those of the past, while its envisaged modality could only underline the absurd untenability of trying to impose capital's ultimate rationality on the recalcitrant parts of the world in that way. Also today, it is quite inconceivable to occupy the whole of China, with its 1,250 million people, and keep it occupied even by the largest economically sustainable outside military force. Not that such inconceivability would deter from their imperialist aims the most extreme adventurists who can envisage no alternative to their world domination; while the "more sober" ones—who in the end are not less dangerous—envisage strategic moves aimed at attempting to break up China, with the help of free market ideology, into fragments controllable from the hegemonic center of global capitalism.

It is self-evident that military forces must be economically sustained, which always confines them to limited enterprises both in the size of the military machines themselves and in the timespan of their operations. The historical record of past imperialist ventures shows that by the time they are vastly extended—as the French first in Indochina and then in Algeria, and later on the United States in Vietnam—the failure of the ventures in question stares them in the face, even if it may take quite some time to disengage from them. With regard to the countless US military imperialist operations of the past, we have to recall not only the Philippines, as well as the failed large-scale war of intervention in Vietnam, [34] but also Guatemala, the Dominican Republic, British Guiana, Grenada, Panama and the Congo, as well as some military operations in other countries, from the Middle East and from the Balkans to various parts of Africa.

One of the most favored ways of enforcing US imperial interests has always been the overthrow of unpalatable governments and the imposition of dictators totally dependent on the new master, so as to rule the countries in question through these well-controlled dictators. Here we are talking about Marcos and Pinochet, Suharto and the Brazilian generals, Somoza and the South Vietnamese puppet generals of the United States, not to forget the Greek colonels (called "sons of a bitch" by Lyndon Johnson) and Seseseko Mobutu (called in a curious sort of praise "our son of a bitch" by a high-ranking State Department official). [35] The contempt with which US government figures ordered about their servants in the countries under their military domination, while cynically representing them for public consumption as champions of the "free world," is clear enough in each case.

2.7

The onset of capital's structural crisis in the 1970s has produced important changes in the posture of imperialism. This is what made it necessary to adopt an increasingly more aggressive and adventurist stand, despite the rhetoric of conciliation, and later

even the absurd propaganda notion of the "new world order," with
its never maintained promise of a "peace dividend." It would be
quite wrong to attribute these changes to the implosion of the
Soviet system, although it is undoubtedly true that the Cold War
and the presumed Soviet military threat was very successfully used
in the past for justifying the unbridled expansion of what General
Eisenhower, toward the end of his presidency, called "the military-
industrial complex." The challenges calling for the adoption of a
more aggressive—and ultimately adventurist—stand were there
well before the collapse of the Soviet system. I described them in
1983 (eight years before the Soviet implosion) as follows:

~ the end of the colonial regime in Mozambique and Angola;

~ the defeat of white racism and the transfer of power to ZANU
in Zimbabwe;

~ the collapse of the US client regime run by the colonels in Greece
and the subsequent victory of Andreas Papandreou's PASOK;

~ the disintegration of Somoza's lifelong, US-backed rule in
Nicaragua and the striking victory of the Sandinista Front;

~ armed liberation struggles in El Salvador and elsewhere in
Central America and the end of the erstwhile easy control of
the region by US imperialism;

~ the total bankruptcy—not only figuratively but also in a literal
sense—of "metropolitan" inspired and dominated "develop-
mental strategies" all over the world, and the eruption of
massive structural contradictions in all three principal industrial powers in Latin America: Argentina, Brazil, and even oil-
rich Mexico;

~ the dramatic and total disintegration of the Shah's regime in Iran
and with it a major defeat of long-established US strategies in
the region, calling into existence *desperately dangerous substitute strategies*—to be implemented *directly or by proxy*—ever since.[36]

What has changed after the collapse of the Soviet system was the need to justify the increasingly more aggressive posture of United States imperialism in different parts of the world. This became especially urgent after the disappointments encountered in trying to revitalize Western capital through the economically sustainable restoration of capitalism—in contrast to the relative but still unstable successes in manipulating the state political machinery through Western "aid"—in the former Soviet Union. The "desperately dangerous substitute strategies implemented directly or by proxy" became prominent in the years preceding and following the Soviet implosion. But the appearance of such dangerous adventurist strategies could not be attributed, as some people think, to the fateful weakening of the Cold War adversary. Rather, the Soviet collapse itself is intelligible only as an integral part of the ongoing structural crisis of the capital system as such.

The Shah as an American proxy—as well as a presumed guarantor against the danger of a new Mossadeq—served his purpose by ruthlessly controlling his people and by buying massive quantities of arms from the West as the means to do so. Once he was gone, another proxy had to be found in order to destroy the antagonist who was talking about the "American Satan." Saddam Hussein's Iraq seemed to fit the bill, armed to the teeth by the United States and other Western countries. But Iraq had failed to destroy Iran and became disposable as an element of instability in a most unstable region of the world from the point of view of US imperialist strategy. Moreover, Saddam Hussein as the former US proxy could now serve a greater purpose. He was promoted to the status of the mythical all-powerful enemy who represents not only the danger attributed in Cold War days to the Soviet Union, but much more than that, someone who threatens with chemical and biological warfare—and also with a nuclear holocaust—the whole of the Western world. Given this mythical enemy, we were expected to justify not only the Gulf War, but also several major military interventions in Iraq since then, as well as the callous killing of one million of its children through the sanctions imposed on the country as a result of US dictates, shamefully accepted by our "great democracies" which continue to boast about their "ethical foreign policies."

But all this is not enough to scratch the surface of the chronic instability even in the region of the Middle East, let alone in the rest of the world. Those who think that present-day imperialism does not require territorial occupation should think again. Military occupation for an indefinite length of time is already in evidence in parts of the Balkans (also admitted to be an "indefinite commitment"), and who can show any reason why similar military territorial occupations should not follow in the future in other parts of the world? The ongoing trends are ominous and the deepening crisis of the system can only make them worse.

In the past we have witnessed two extremely dangerous developments in the ideology and organizational framework of US imperialism. First, NATO has not only expanded significantly toward the east, which may be considered by the Russian authorities a threat, if not today then some time in the future. Even more importantly, the aims and objectives of NATO have been radically redefined, in conflict with international law, transforming it from what used to be a supposedly purely defensive military association into a potentially most aggressive offensive alliance, which can do what it pleases without any reference to lawful authority—or, rather, it can do what the United States pleases and orders it to do. At the April 1999 NATO summit in Washington the North Atlantic Treaty Organization, under American pressure, "adopted a new strategic concept, by which they said they can resort to military action even outside the NATO area, without caring about the sovereignty of other countries and in disregard of the United Nations."[37] What is also highly significant in this respect is that the ideological justification of the new, unmistakably aggressive, posture—offered in the form of twenty-four "risk factors"—is transparently shaky. It has even been admitted that "out of the twenty-four risk factors only five can be considered to represent real military danger."[38]

The second recent development, which is especially dangerous, concerns the new Japan-US Security Treaty. This treaty has been characteristically railroaded through the Japanese houses of parliament (the Diet and the upper house of Counsellors). It has been almost completely ignored in the West, sadly even on the left.[39] In this case too, the new developments cynically defy international law, and also violate the Japanese constitution. As an important Japanese political leader, Tetsuzo Fuwa, commented: "The dangerous nature of the Japan-US Security Treaty has evolved to the extent of possibly dragging Japan into US wars, challenging the Japanese Constitution which renounces war. Behind this is the extremely dangerous US preventive strike strategy by which the United States will interfere in another country and arbitrarily attack any country it dislikes."[40] It goes without saying that the role assigned to Japan in the "preventive strike strategy," in which the orders emanate from Washington, is that of "cannon fodder." At the same time Japan is expected to contribute generously to the financial costs of military operations, as they were compelled to do also in the case of the Gulf War.[41]

One of the most sinister aspects of these developments came to light recently when Japanese Vice Defense Minister Shingo Nishimura was forced to resign for "jumping the gun" and aggressively advocating that Japan should arm itself with nuclear weapons. And he went even further, projecting in an interview the use of military force, with reference to the disputed Senkaku Islands. He declared "Should diplomacy fail to settle the dispute, the Defence Agency will tackle it." As an editorial article of the journal *Akahata* pointed out:

The real problem here is that a politician who openly argued for the nuclear armament of Japan and the use of military force as means to solve international disputes was given a cabinet seat. It is natural that other Asian nations have expressed grave concern over the matter. What is more, under a secret agreement with the US government, LDP governments have gutted the three non-nuclear principles (not to possess, manufacture, or allow nuclear weapons to be brought into Japan). Moreover, the recent "emergency legislation" is aimed at giving military operations by the US forces and the SDF [Self-Defense Force] priority in the event of war by mobilizing for war cooperation, commandeering commodities, land sites, buildings, and controlling ships, aircraft and electric waves. Such legislation will undermine the Constitution.[42]

Naturally, the new aggressive posture of the Japan-US Security Treaty is justified in the name of the necessities of Japanese defense. In truth, however, the "Common Defense" claimed in the legitimating report (quoted in note 41) has nothing to do with "defending Japan" against a fictitious aggressor, but everything to do with the protection and enhancement of US imperialist interests.

The US use their bases in Japan, including those in Okinawa, to carry out military intervention in politically unstable situations in South East Asian countries, including Indonesia. In May last year, when the Suharto regime went down in Indonesia, US Army Special Forces units suddenly returned to the US Torii Station in Yomitan village, Okinawa, via US Kadena Base in Okinawa. They had trained the special forces of the Indonesian Armed Forces (ABRI) which suppressed demonstrations in the country. The sudden return of the US Army Special units Forces indicated the secret activity that US Green Beret units in Okinawa had engaged in Indonesia.[43]

These dangerous policies and practices are imposed on the countries whose "democratic" governments meekly submit to all US dictates. As a rule the changes are not even discussed in the respective parliaments, bypassing them instead through secret treaties and protocols. And in the same spirit of cynical evasion, when for some reason they appear on the parliamentary agenda, they are bulldozed through, dismissing all opposition in the most authoritarian fashion. The politicians who in this way continue to "sow dragon seeds" seem to be oblivious to the danger of real dragons appearing on the historical stage in due course. Nor do they seem to understand or admit that the devastating flame of the nuclear dragons is not confined to a given locality—the Middle East or Far East, for instance—but can engulf absolutely everything on this planet, including the United States and Europe.

2.8

The ultimate target of the projected US preventive strikes strategy is, of course, China. Commenting on the aggressive noises and leaks in Washington against China in the aftermath of the bombing of the Chinese embassy in Belgrade, Rear Admiral Eugene Carroll, of the Center for Defense Information, an independent think-tank, said: "There is a demonization of China going on here. I am not sure who is doing it, but these leaks are orchestrated to show China as the *yellow peril*."[44]

The bombing of the Chinese embassy in Belgrade was at first presented and justified by NATO spokesmen as an "inevitable, even if regrettable, accident." When later it became undeniable that the embassy was not hit by a stray bomb but by rockets from three different directions, hence a carefully targeted attack, Washington produced a fairy-tale explanation: that the CIA could not obtain an up-to-date map of Belgrade, available to everybody else in any corner shop. But even then the mystery remained complete as to what was so important and legitimate about the building that was once sup- posed to have occupied the space filled by the Chinese embassy or what made it a legitimate target. We are still waiting for some credible answers, which will obviously never come. A rational explanation that comes to mind is that the operation was designed as a testing ground, in two respects. First, it was a test of the way the Chinese government would respond to such acts of aggression, compelling it to swallow the humiliation that went with them. And second, perhaps more importantly, it was a test of world public opinion, which proved to be utterly meek and compliant.

The problems deeply affecting US-China relations could not be more serious. In one sense they arise from the inconvenient fact that *"the party-state has still not found a place in the free market world."*[45] When global hegemonic imperialism uses as its ideological legitimation the concepts of "democracy" and "free market" any departure from such an ideology—backed by a major economic and military power—represents a serious challenge. And what makes the challenge quite intolerable is the prospect of economic developments to the disadvantage of the United States, given the comparable present rates of expansion, coupled with the fact that China's population is greater than that of the United States by a staggering *one thousand million*. As the same article puts it, reflecting great concerns about the ongoing developments: *"By 2020 China's economy alone would be three times that of the United States"*[46] It is not too difficult to imagine the alarm raised by such prospects in US ruling circles.

True to its apologetic role, the *Economist* tries to put a glaze of respectability on this advocacy of military readiness and preparedness to die for "democracy" and the "free market." In an article on "the new geopolitics" it calls for the acceptance of piling up body bags. The United States will not be called upon to fill these bags, of course. Dead bodies were to be provided by what the *Economist* calls the "local assistants" of the United States. With boundless hypocrisy the *Economist* speaks of a necessary "moral commitment" to war by the democracies, asking them in the name of that morality to accept that "war is a time of dying as well as of killing."

To be the devoted "local assistant" of the United States is the role assigned to Japan, justified in view of the projected Chinese threat. The serious opposition in the country to the redefined and dangerously expanded Japan-US Security Treaty is characterized as "nervousness." Happily, China will make the Japanese see sense and strengthen their resolve. For "A growing China will also make a nervous Japan readier to cling to its alliance with America." The same role of a devoted local assistant is assigned to Turkey and, expressing the Economist's hope, also to India, arguing that "the armies of allied countries whose people do not mind their soldiers doing the face-to-face work [i.e. dying] may come to the rescue; this is why Turkey matters to the alliance,[47] and why one day it may be a good idea to ask for India's help." In this scheme of things Russia, too, will occupy an actively pro-American place, thanks to its projected unavoidable opposition to China. "Worried about the vulnerability of its eastern territories, Russia may at last choose to put some substance into its flimsy Partnership-for-Peace links with NATO." The characterization of countries as "nervous" and "worried"—if not today then tomorrow—is all on account of their expected conflicts with "the rising giant of the East," China. In the "new geopolitics," China is presented as the common denominator of all trouble, and simultaneously also as the solution cementing all the "worried" and "nervous" into an "Alliance for Democracy" and a "Partnership-for-Peace,"[48] which "might even draw a democratic India [a traditionally non-aligned country] into a new, South Asian version of the Partnership-for-Peace" under the United States. We are not told, however, that we shall live happily ever after, or indeed live at all.

Naturally, this kind of "doctrine," inspired by Washington, is not confined to the London Economist. It had found its spokesmen also in the Far East, where Australia's Prime Minister, John Howard, proclaimed the "Howard doctrine" according to which his own

country should fulfill the role of the faithful US "local assistant."
To the consternation of Southeast Asian political opinion he de-
clared "Australia will act as the United States' 'deputy sheriff' in
regional peace-keeping."[49] Malaysia's opposition leader, Lim Kit
Siang, responded to this idea by saying that "Mr. Howard had done
more than any previous Australian Prime Minister to damage
Australia's relations with Asia since the 'White Australia' policy was
abolished in the 1960s."[50] Hadi Soesastro, an American-educated
Indonesian academic, hit the head of the nail by pointing out that
"It is always the deputy sheriff who gets killed."[51] Indeed, that is
precisely the role of the US "local assistants": to kill and to get
killed for the cause handed down to them from above.

Marx wrote in his *Eighteenth Brumaire of Louis Bonaparte* that historical
events often appear twice, in contrasting forms: first, as a (Napole-
onic) *tragedy,* and later as the *farce of Napoléon le petit.* The role assigned to
Japan in the recently revised, unconstitutional Japan-US Security
Treaty could only produce a major tragedy in Southeast Asia, and an
equally tragic devastation to Japan itself. The muscle-flexing "US
deputy sheriff" role proclaimed in the Howard doctrine can only be
described as the farce eagerly running ahead of the tragedy.

2.9

The history of imperialism has three distinct phases:

1. *Early modern colonial empire-building imperialism,* brought about
through the expansion of some European countries in the relatively easily penetrable parts of the world;

2. *"Redistributive" imperialism, antagonistically contested by the major powers
on behalf of their quasi-monopolistic corporations,* called by Lenin "the
highest stage of capitalism," involving only a few real contenders,
and some smaller survivors from the past hanging on to their
coattails, coming to an end in the immediate aftermath of the
Second World War; and

3. *Global hegemonic imperialism*, with the United States as its overpowering force, foreshadowed by Roosevelt's version of the "open door" policy, with its pretenses of democratic equity. This third phase was consolidated soon after the Second World War, and became sharply pronounced with the onset of the capital system's structural crisis in the 1970s, when the imperative to constitute the all-embracing political command structure of capital under a "global government" presided over by the globally dominant country became pressing.

Those who entertained the illusion that postwar "neo-colonialism" had brought into being a stable system in which political/military domination had been replaced by straightforward economic domination tended to assign too much weight to the continued power of the former colonial imperialist masters after the formal dissolution of their empires, underrating at the same time the exclusionary aspirations of global US hegemonic domination and the causes sustaining them. They imagined that by setting up institutes of development studies—for the purpose of "further educating" the postcolonial political and administrative elites of their former dependencies, inducing them to adopt the newly promoted theories and policies of "modernization" and "development"—the former colonial rulers could secure a substantive continuity with their old system. What had put an end to such illusions was not only the overwhelmingly greater power of penetration of the American corporations (forcefully backed by the US government) but, even more, the collapse of the whole policy of modernization everywhere, as discussed above.

The fact that US hegemonic imperialism proved to be so successful, and still continues to prevail, does not mean that it can be considered stable, let alone permanent. The envisaged "global government" under US management remains wishful thinking, like the "Alliance for Democracy" and the "Partnership for Peace," projected—at a time of multiplying military collisions and social explosions—as the solid foundation of the newest version of the "new world order." We have been there before—after the implosion of the Soviet system—when such vision

> Found favor in a US anxious to keep the capitalist dynamo going at the end of the Cold War. Selective engagement with key "emerging market" states provided an alternative foreign policy to the defunct containment strategy. The policy envisaged the United States at the hub of "One World" driving toward shared prosperity, democracy and better living conditions for all. Western corporations would pour technologies into the poorer regions of the world, where labor was abundant, cheap and talented. Global financial markets, no longer under political lock and key, would provide capital. Within a couple of decades, there would arise a huge transnational market for consumers.[52]

Over ten years of the projected couple of decades are over, and we are in a much worse condition than ever before even in an advanced capitalist country like Britain, where—according to the latest statistics—*one in three children* lives below the poverty line, and in the last twenty years their numbers *multiplied threefold*. And no one should have illusions about how the structural crisis of capital affects even the richest country, the United States. For there too conditions deteriorated greatly in the last two decades. According to a recent report of the Congressional Budget Office—and no one could accuse that office of a left-wing bias—the richest *one percent* of the population earns as much as the bottom 100 million (i.e. nearly *forty percent*). And significantly, this appalling number has *doubled since 1977*, when the top one percent's income was equivalent to that of "only" 49 million of the poorest, i.e. less than *twenty percent* of the population.[53]

As to the rest of the optimistic projections quoted above, no longer are we treated to the mirage of "a huge transnational market" bringing "prosperity to all," including the people in the

East. The Chinese Prime Minister, Zhu Rongji, is now praised for his "bold attempts to bring reform to the state sector, which now means *unemployment for millions of Chinese workers.*"[54] How many more millions of workers—or indeed hundreds of millions of them—must be made unemployed before it can be said that China has finally qualified "for a place in the free market world"? For the time being the editorial of the *Economist* can only express its hope, and prognosticate its realization, that the Chinese system will be overthrown from inside,[55] and project the external military solution in other articles, as we have seen above. What is common to the two approaches is the complete absence of any sense of reality. For even if the Chinese system could be overthrown today or tomorrow, that would solve absolutely nothing as regards the total failure of the sanguine expectations once attached to the "emergent market states" and their projected impact "to keep the capitalist dynamo going at the end of the Cold War."

In the meantime the contradictions and antagonisms remain ineradicable and continue to intensify. Under the rule of capital, which is *structurally* incapable of resolving its contradictions—hence its way of *postponing* the moment of truth, until the accumulated pressures result in some kind of explosion—there is a tendency to misrepresent historical time, in the direction of both the past and the future, in the interest of eternalizing the present. The tendentious misreading of the past arises from the ideological imperative to misrepresent the present as the necessary structural framework of all possible change. For precisely because the established present must be timelessly projected into the future, the past must also be fictionalized—in the form of a projection backwards—as the domain of the system's eternal presence in another form, so as to remove the actual historical determinations and the time-bound limitations of the present.

As a result of the perverse interests at the roots of capital's relation to time, it can have neither a long-term perspective, nor a sense of urgency even when an explosion is about to take place. Enterprises are oriented toward, and their success is measured in, the fulfillment of projections conceived on the most myopic timescale. This is why the intellectuals who adopt the standpoint of capital like to argue that whatever worked in the past—encapsulated in the idealized method of doing "little by little"—is bound to work also in the future. This is a dangerous fallacy. For time is not on our side, given the accumulating pressure of our contradictions. The projection of the *Economist* about the happy alignment of all the "nervous" and "worried" countries with US strategies is, at best, an arbitrary projection of the present into the future, if not a complete misrepresentation of present realities in order to make them suit the wishfully anticipated future. For even the present-day contradictions between the United States and Japan, as well as between Russia and the United States, are much greater than the adopted scheme of things allows for, not to mention their potential unfolding in the future. Nor should one ignore the objective conflicts of interest between India and the United States in order to transfigure them into perfect harmony on account of the postulated "nervousness" about China.

Moreover, even the apparently prevalent harmony of the United States with the European Union in the framework of NATO should not be taken for granted to persist in the future, given the clear signs of inter-imperialist conflicts both within the EU and between the EU and the United States.[56] At times even the *Economist* gives away its concern that not everything is going as it should in the conflict-ridden power relations of the West, although insisting that no one should even dream about challenging US domination. As an editorial article of the journal puts it:

> Even the motives for a common foreign policy vary. Some Euro-
> peans want it as an expression of Europe's common political will;

others as a rival to, and restraint upon, the United States. If it turned into nothing more than a form of anti-Americanism, it would be a disaster. For the foreseeable future, NATO, preferably in synch with the UN, will be the linchpin of western security. America must still take the lead in dealing with most of the world's danger zones. But in near-at-hand places like the Balkans, America will happily defer to Europe. And even in areas like the Middle East or Russia, Europe ought to be able to play a complementary role to America. Europe can and should exercise a greater influence in the world, but it will not be a superpower for many years yet.[57]

The meaningless phrase "Europe can and should exercise a greater influence in the world" (like what? and where?) is thrown in as an empty consolation prize, so as to legitimate in the eyes of the feeble-minded the absolute supremacy of the United States, propagandized by the Economist. In truth, however, the question is not at all How long will it take for Europe to become a "superpower" matching the military might of the United States? Rather: In what form and with what intensity will the simmering inter-imperialist antagonisms erupt into the open in that by no means distant future?

As a matter of fact, the US administration has been quite concerned about the prospects of European developments.

> Strobe Talbot, former deputy Secretary of State, said, the last thing Washington wanted to see was a European defense identity "which begins within NATO, but grows out of NATO, and then away from NATO." The risk, he told a seminar at the Royal Institute of International Affairs, is of an EU defense structure that "first duplicates the alliance and then competes with the alliance." Mr Talbot's words ... also touch America's basic ambivalence about greater European unity: that it is fine *so long as it does not threaten US global pre-eminence*.[58]

Thus the US State Department misses no opportunity to hammer home the plain truth about its determination to keep the rest of the world subservient to the demands of its *"global pre-eminence."* Naturally, the most subservient of all Western governments, the British, hastened to oblige and voice its unqualified reassurance at the same seminar of the Royal Institute of International Affairs. "Trying to allay US anxieties, Lord George Robertson, the outgoing Secretary of State for Defense who takes over at NATO from Xavier Solana next week, declared that the Atlantic alliance remains the cornerstone of British defense policy."[59] That may be so, for as long as the "Trojan horse" role assigned by the United States to the British government in Europe remains unquestioned. However, such reassurances are no more than whistling in the dark as regards the existing objective contradictions of interest among the Western powers, which are bound to intensify in the future, no matter how forcefully the US State Department reminds the EU of who is really entitled to call the tune even when refusing to pay for it.

# 3. HISTORICAL CHALLENGES FACING
# THE SOCIALIST MOVEMENT

## 3.1

As we have seen earlier, the anti-imperialist movement in the United States at the turn of the nineteenth to twentieth century failed because of labor's "conciliation with the trusts and support for their foreign policy." The conclusion of Lincoln's former associate, George S. Boutwell, in 1902, that "The final effort for the salvation of the republic is to be made by the laboring and producing classes" sounds prophetic today. For the conditions of success remain the same, and only the American "laboring and producing classes" can bring to an end the destructive drive of global hegemonic imperialism. No political/military power on earth can accomplish from the *outside* what must be done from *inside* by a movement offering a positive alternative to the existing order in the United States.

Naturally, this does not mean that everyone else can sit back and wait until the required action is over, because it can never be completed in isolation. The problems and contradictions are so inextricably intertwined that their solution requires profound changes also in other parts of the world. The deep-seated causes of the explosive contradictions must be addressed everywhere, through the commitment of a truly international enterprise whose particular constituents confront their own share of capital's jungle-like network of contradictions, in solidarity with the "laboring and producing classes" in America and elsewhere in the world. American labor's "conciliation with the trusts and support for their foreign policy" at the turn of the century[60] was due, on the one hand, to the availability of outlets for imperialist expansion and thereby the postponing displacement of capital's contradictions; and on the side of labor, to the absence of the objective and subjective conditions[61] of a *viable hegemonic alternative* to capital's mode of controlling societal reproduction. Such an alternative is inconceivable without international solidarity oriented toward the creation of an order of substantive equality.

One does not have to be a militant socialist to realize the dangers we face. It is relevant to recall in this context the alarm raised in 1997 by Nobel Prize winner Joseph Rotblat concerning the profit-driven research activities pursued in the field of biotechnology and "cloning." As we know, under the rule of capital such activities—entrapped by the system's expansionary imperatives, whatever the human and environmental consequences—represent a new dimension of humanity's potential self-destruction. This new dimension is now being added to the already existing arsenal of nuclear, chemical and biological weapons: each capable of inflicting on us a universal holocaust many times over.

Denis Noble, a distinguished liberal scientist who was most prominent in the protest movement that prevented Margaret Thatcher's election to the chancellorship of Oxford University, extended Rotblat's argument to point out the danger of uncontrollable and potentially self-destructive ways in which scientific knowledge is produced and utilized in our social order. He wrote in a recent paper on academic integrity:

The structures of society—social, political, religious—are creaking heavily with our inability to absorb what we know into ethical and social systems that are capable of being widely accepted. The problem is urgent. . . . One possible outcome is, of course, a retreat into fundamentalism of various forms, which would certainly challenge academic integrity severely. The alternative is to acknowledge that there is an obligation on the part of the creators of this stockpile of knowledge to work out *how to disarm its ability to destroy us.*[62]

The social responsibility of scientists for fighting against such dangers cannot be overstated. Indeed, the scientists who took part in this enterprise in the twentieth century included some of their greatest. Thus Einstein, for instance, conducted for many years his struggle against the militarization of science and for the vital cause of nuclear disarmament. In a message he drafted for a planned—but, as a result of gross interference, never actually convened—national congress of scientists, Einstein wrote:

I am sincerely gratified that the great majority of scientists are fully conscious of their responsibilities as scholars and world citizens; and that they have not fallen victim to the widespread hysteria that threatens our future and that of our children. It is horrifying to realize that the poison of militarism and imperialism threatens to bring undesirable changes in the political attitude of the United States ... What we see at work here is not an expression of the sentiments of the American people; rather, it reflects the will of a powerful minority which uses its economic power to control the organs of political life. Should the government pursue this fateful course, we scientists must refuse to submit to its immoral demands, even if they are backed by legal machinery. There is an unwritten law, that of our own conscience, which is far more binding than any bills that may be devised in Washington. And there are, of course, even for us, the ultimate weapons: non-cooperation and strike.[63]

The cancellation of the meeting, scheduled for January 10–12, 1946, disappointed Einstein's publicly declared belief in the consciously accepted social responsibility of the great majority of scientists. Nevertheless, he continued his struggle until he died, defying threats and public denunciations. He knew very well that "men have never freed themselves from intolerable bondage, frozen into law, except by revolutionary action,"[64] and he insisted that "Deeds, not words are needed; mere words get pacifists nowhere. They must initiate action and begin with what can be achieved now."[65] Yet, despite his immense prestige and quite unparalleled access to heads of governments as well as to the media, Einstein was in the end completely isolated and defeated by the political apologists of the growing military/industrial complex. They even called for his prosecution,[66] with a view to expulsion from the United States, with a Mississippi delegate thundering in Congress, "This foreign-born agitator would have us plunge into another European war in order to further the spread of Communism throughout the world."[67]

Thus, even the protest of the century's greatest socially concerned and politically conscious scientist had to remain a cry in the wilderness. For it was not amplified by a *mass movement* that could confront and disarm the deeply entrenched destructive forces of capital through its own practically viable alternative vision of how to order human affairs. Boutwell presented such an alternative when he insisted that "The final effort for the salvation of the republic"—as against the empire-building, adventurist big corporations and their state—"is to be made by the laboring and producing classes." Boutwell uttered these words nearly a century ago, and their truth has been intensifying ever since. For the dangers have immeasurably increased for the whole of humanity, not only compared to 1902, when Boutwell spoke, but even in comparison to Einstein's time. The megatons in the nuclear arsenal, which worried Einstein, have not only multiplied since the time of his death, but also proliferated, despite all self-deluding talk about the "end of the Cold War." We were reminded of the real state of affairs quite recently when President Yeltsin tried to justify the "sovereign right" of his country's gruesome war against Chechnya by warning the rest of the world that Russia still possessed a full arsenal of nuclear weapons.

Today, in addition to the nuclear threat of MAD ("Mutually Assured Destruction"), the knowledge of how to employ chemical and biological weaponry in the service of mass extermination is at the disposal of all those who would not hesitate to use such weapons if the rule of capital was threatened. And that is by no means all. For by now environmental destruction, in the service of capital's blindly pursued interests, has assumed such proportions that even if the process is reversed tomorrow, it would take decades to produce any significant change in this respect by neutralizing capital's pernicious self propelling and self sustaining articulation, which must pursue its "rational," and in immediate terms "economic," *line of least resistance.* The scale of this destruction is dramatically illustrated by the terrible calamity inflicted in the dying days of the twentieth century on the people of Venezuela, as a result of irresponsible deforestation and speculative "development." Moreover, the potentially lethal implications of tampering with nature through recklessly used biotechnology, cloning, and through the uncontrolled genetic modification of food products, under the dictates of profit-seeking giant corporations and their governments, represent the opening of a new Pandora's box.

These are the clearly visible dangers on our horizon, as things stand today; and who knows what additional dangers will appear through capital's destructive uncontrollability for our children's tomorrow! However, what in the light of our historical experience is absolutely clear is that only a genuine socialist mass movement can counter and defeat the forces that are now pushing humankind toward the abyss of self-destruction.

## 3.2

The urgently needed constitution of the radical alternative to capital's mode of social metabolic reproduction cannot take place without a critical reexamination of the past. It is necessary to examine the failure of the historical left to live up to Marx's optimistic expectation in 1847 that the trade unionist "combination" and ensuing political development of the working class would take place in close parallel to the industrial development of the various capitalist countries. As he put it:

> The degree to which combination has developed in any country clearly marks the rank it occupies in the hierarchy of the world market. England, whose industry has attained the highest degree of development, has the biggest and best-organized combinations. In England they have not stopped at *partial combinations* . . . they went on simultaneously with the political struggles of the workers, who now constitute a large political party, under the name of the *Chartists*. [68]

Marx expected this process to continue in such a way that

> The working class, in the course of its development, will substitute for the old civil society an association which will exclude classes and their antagonism, and *there will be no more political power properly so called*, since political power is precisely the official expression of antagonism in civil society. [69]

However, the historical development of the working class was characterized by ongoing partiality and sectionality. These characteristics were not confined to "partial combinations" and to the various trade unions that arose from them. Inevitably at first, partiality affected every aspect of the socialist movement, including its political dimension. So much so, in fact, that a century and a half later it still presents an immense problem, to be resolved some time in the hopefully not very distant future.

The labor movement could not help being sectional and partial in its beginnings. This was not simply a question of subjectively adopting the wrong strategy, as often claimed, but a matter of objective determinations. As mentioned earlier, the "plurality of capitals" could not and cannot be overcome within the framework of capital's social metabolic order, despite the overpowering tendency toward the monopolistic concentration and centralization—as well as the transnational, but precisely in its transnational (and not genuinely multinational) character necessarily partial development—of globalizing capital. At the same time, the "plurality of labor," too, cannot be superseded on capital's ground of social metabolic reproduction, no matter how much effort is invested in trying to turn labor from capital's structurally irreconcilable antagonist into its uniformly compliant servant; attempts ranging from the mystifying and absurd propaganda of shareholding "people's capitalism" to the all-embracing direct political extraction of surplus labor exercised by the post-capitalist personifications of capital who tried to legitimate themselves through their spurious claim to be the embodiment of the true interests of the working class.

The sectional and partial character of the labor movement was combined with its *defensive* articulation. Early trade unionism—from which the political parties later emerged—represented the tendentially authoritarian *centralization of sectionality*, and thereby the transfer of the power of decision making from the local "combinations" to the trade union centers, and subsequently to the political parties. Thus already the early trade union movement as a whole was inevitably *sectional and defensive*. Indeed, due to the inner logic of development of this movement, the *centralization of sectionality* carried with it the *entrenchment of defensiveness* as compared to the sporadic attacks through which the local combinations could inflict serious damage on their local capital antagonists. (The more distant Luddite relatives tried to do the same in a more generalized destructive, and therefore within a very short run of time quite unviable form.) The entrenchment of defensiveness thus represented a paradoxical historical advance. For through its early trade unions labor became also the *interlocutor* of capital, without ceasing to be objectively its structural antagonist. From this new position of labor's generalized defensiveness certain advantages could be derived, *under favorable conditions*, for some sections of labor. This was possible so long as the corresponding constituents of capital could adjust themselves on a countrywide scale—in tune with the dynamic of potential capital expansion and accumulation—to the demands conveyed to them by the defensively articulated labor movement. This movement operated within the structural premises of the capital system, as a legally constituted and state-regulated interlocutor. The development of the welfare state was the ultimate manifestation of this logic, workable in a very limited number of countries. It was limited both as regards the *favorable conditions* of undisturbed capital expansion in the countries concerned, as the precondition of the welfare state's appearance, and in relation to its time scale, marked in the end by the "radical right" pressure for the complete liquidation of the welfare state in the last three decades, as a result of the structural crisis of the capital system as a whole.

With the constitution of labor's political parties—in the form of the separation of the "industrial arm" of labor (the trade unions) from its "political arm" (the social-democratic and the vanguardist parties)—the defensiveness of the movement was further entrenched. For both types of parties appropriated for themselves the exclusive right of overall decision making, which was already foreshadowed in the centralized sectionality of the trade union movements themselves. This defensiveness was rendered worse still through the mode of operation adopted by the political parties, obtaining certain successes at the cost of derailing and diverting the socialist movement from its original objectives.

For in the capitalist parliamentary framework, in exchange for the acceptance by capital of the legitimacy of labor's political parties, it became quite unlawful to use the "industrial arm" for political purposes. This amounted to a severely constraining condition to which the parties of labor consented, thereby condemning the immense combative potential of materially rooted and potentially also politically most effective productive labor to total powerlessness. Acting in this way was all the more problematical since capital, through its structurally secured supremacy, remained the *extra-parliamentary force par excellence*, which could dominate parliament as it pleased from the outside. Nor could the situation be considered any better for labor in post-capitalist countries. For Stalin degraded the trade unions to the status of being what he called the "transmission belts" of official propaganda, exempting simultaneously the post-capitalist political form of authoritarian decision making from any possibility of control by the working class base. Understandably, therefore, in view of our unhappy historical experience with both main types of political parties, there can be no hope for the radical re-articulation of the socialist movement without fully combining labor's *"industrial arm" with its "political arm"*: by conferring the power of meaningful political decision making on the trade unions (thus encouraging them to be directly political), on the one hand, and by making the political parties themselves defiantly active in industrial conflicts as the uncompromising antagonists of capital, assuming responsibility for their struggle *inside and outside* parliament.

The labor movement throughout its long history remained sectional and defensive. Indeed, these two defining characteristics constituted a veritable vicious circle. Labor in its divided and often internally torn plurality could not break out of its paralyzing sectional constraints, in dependency to the plurality of capitals, because it was articulated defensively as a general movement; and vice versa, it could not overcome the grave limitations of its necessary defensiveness vis-à-vis capital, because up to the present time it remained sectional in its organized industrial and political articulation. At the same time, to make the vicious circle even tighter, the defensive role assumed by labor conferred a strange form of legitimacy on capital's mode of social metabolic control. For, by default, labor's defensive posture explicitly or tacitly consented to treating the established socioeconomic and political order as the necessary framework of, and the continuing prerequisite to, what could be considered "realistically feasible" out of the advocated demands, demarcating at the same time the only legitimate way of resolving the conflicts that would arise from the rival claims of the interlocutors. This amounted to a kind of self-censorship, much to the delight of capital's eager personifications. It represented a numbing *self-censorship*, resulting in a strategic inactivity that continues to paralyze even the more radical remnants of the organized historical left, not to mention its once upon a time genuinely reformist but by now totally tamed and integrated constituents.

So long as the defensive posture of capital's "rational interlocutor"—whose rationality was defined *a priori* by what could be fitted into the practical premises and constraints of the ruling order—could produce relative gains for labor, the self-proclaimed *legitimacy* of capital's overall political regulatory framework remained fundamentally unchallenged. Once under the pressure of its structural crisis, however, capital could not yield anything of significance to its "rational interlocutor" but, on the contrary, had to take back also its past concessions, ruthlessly attacking the very foundations of the welfare state as well as labor's protective/defensive legal safeguards through a set of "democratically enacted" authoritarian anti-trade union laws. In this way, the legitimacy of the established political order was eroded, exposing at the same time the total untenability of labor's defensive posture.

The "*crisis of politics*" cannot be denied today even by the system's worst apologists. Of course, they try to confine it to the sphere of political manipulation and its unholy consensus, in the spirit of New Labour's "third way." But this crisis of politics represents a profound *crisis of legitimacy* of the established mode of social metabolic reproduction and its overall framework of political control. This is what has brought with it the *historical actuality of the socialist offensive*,[70] even if labor's pursuit of its own "line of least resistance" continues to favor for the time being the maintenance of the existing order, despite that order's more and more obvious failure to "deliver the goods"—even in the most advanced capitalist countries—as the ground of its once overwhelmingly accepted legitimacy. "New Labour" today, in all of its European varieties, is the facilitator for "delivering the goods" only to the entrenched capital interests, whether in the domain of finance capital cynically championed by the Blair government even in conflict with some of its European partners—or some industrial and quasi-monopolistic commercial sections of it. At the same time, in order to defend the system under the conditions of capital's narrowing margins of reproductive viability, the concerns of the working class are totally ignored. Thus capital's vital interests are facilitated by retaining all of the authoritarian anti-labor legislation of the recent past,[71] and by using the power of the state to support capital's push for the massive *casualization* of the labor force, as a cynically deceptive "solution" of the unemployment problem. This is why the need for a socialist offensive cannot be removed from the historical agenda by any given or conceivable variety of labor's defensive accommodation.

It should be of no surprise that under the present conditions of crisis the siren song of Keynesianism is heard again as a wishful remedy, appealing to the spirit of the old "expansionary consensus" in the service of "development." However, today that song can only sound as something very faint, emerging through a long pipe from the bottom of a very deep Keynesian grave. For the type of consensus cultivated by the existing varieties of accommodated labor in reality has to make palatable the *structural failure* of capital expansion and accumulation, in sharp contrast to the conditions that once enabled Keynesian policies to prevail for a very limited historical period. Luigi Vinci, a prominent figure in the Italian *Rifondazione* movement, rightly stressed that today the proper self-definition and autonomous organizational viability of the radical socialist forces is "often badly hindered by a vague and optimistic left-Keynesianism in which the central position is occupied by the magic word 'development.' "[72] Even at the peak of Keynesian expansion this notion of "development" could not bring one inch nearer the socialist alternative, because it always took for granted the necessary practical premises of capital as the orienting framework of its own strategy, firmly under the internalized constraints of the "line of least resistance."

It must also be stressed that Keynesianism is by its very nature conjunctural. Since it operates within capital's structural parameters, it cannot help being *conjunctural*, irrespective of whether the prevailing circumstances favor a shorter or a longer conjuncture. Keynesianism, even in its "left-Keynesian" variety, is necessarily situated within, and constrained by, capital's *stop-go logic*. Even at its best Keynesianism can represent nothing more than the "go" phase of an expansionary cycle, which sooner or later must be brought to an end by the "stop" phase. In its origins Keynesianism tried to offer an alternative to this stop-go logic, by managing both phases in a "balanced" way. However, it failed to do so, remaining instead tied to the one-sided "go" phase, due to the very nature of its capitalist state-oriented regulatory framework. The quite unusual length of postwar Keynesian expansion—but even that confined, significantly, to a handful of advanced capitalist coun-

tries—was largely due to the favorable conditions of postwar reconstruction and to the dominant position assumed in it by the overwhelmingly state-financed military-industrial complex. On the other
hand, the fact that the corrective-counteracting "stop" phase had to
acquire the exceptionally harsh and callous form of "neo-liberalism"
(and "monetarism" as its pseudo-objective ideological rationalization)—already under Harold Wilson's Labour government, whose
monetarist financial policy was presided over by Denis Healy, as
Chancellor of the Exchequer—was due to the onset of capital's (no
longer traditionally cyclic) *structural crisis*, embracing an entire historical epoch. This is what explains the exceptional duration of the
neo-liberal "stop" phase, by now much longer than the postwar
Keynesian "go" phase. And there is no end in sight yet, as it is
perpetuated under the watchful eyes of Conservative and Labour
governments alike.

Both the anti-labor harshness and the frightening duration of the
neo-liberal stop phase, together with the fact that neo-liberalism is
practiced by governments that were supposed to be situated on the
opposite sides of the parliamentary political divide, are in reality
intelligible only as the manifestations of capital's structural crisis. The
brutal longevity of the neo-liberal phase is ideologically rationalized
by some laborite theoreticians as the "downward long cycle" of
normal capitalist development, which is certain to be followed by
another "expansionary long cycle." This circumstance only underlines the complete failure of reformist "strategic thinking" to grasp
the nature of the ongoing trends of development. For the savagery of
neo-liberalism continues its course, quite unchallenged by accommodated labor, and we are now running out of the years predicated
even by the fanciful notion of the coming "positive long cycle" as
theorized by capital's laborite apologists.

Thus, given the structural crisis of the capital system, even if a
conjunctural shift could bring back for a while an attempt to

institute some form of Keynesian state financial management, that could be done only for an extremely limited duration, due to the absence of the material conditions that would favor its extension for a longer time even in the dominant capitalist countries. More importantly still, such limited conjunctural revival could offer absolutely nothing for the realization of a radical socialist alternative. For it would be impossible to build a viable strategic alternative to capital's mode of social metabolic control on an internal conjunctural way of managing the system, a way that needs the healthy expansion and accumulation of capital as the necessary precondition of its own mode of operation.

### 3.3

As we have seen in the last few pages, the sectional limitations and defensiveness of labor could not be overcome through the movement's trade unionist and political centralization. This historical failure is now strongly underlined by capital's transnational globalization to which labor does not seem to have any answer.

It must be recalled here that in the course of the last century and a half no less than four Internationals have been founded in an attempt to create the required international unity of labor. However, all four of them failed even to approximate their stated objectives, let alone to realize them. This cannot be made intelligible simply in terms of personal betrayals. Even if these terms are accurate at a personal level, they still beg the question and ignore the weighty objective determinations that must be kept in mind if we want to remedy the situation in the future. For it remains to be explained why the circumstances actually favored such derailments and betrayals over a very long historical period.

The fundamental problem is that the sectional plurality of labor is closely linked to the hierarchically structured conflictual plurality of capitals, both within every particular country and on a global scale. If it were not for the latter, it would be much easier to envisage the successful constitution of labor's international unity against unified or unifiable capital. However, given the necessarily hierarchical/conflictual articulation of the capital system, with its incorrigibly iniquitous internal and international pecking order, the global unity of capital—to which in principle the corresponding international unity of labor could be unproblematically counterposed—is not feasible. The much deplored historical fact that in major international conflicts the working classes of the various countries sided with their countrywide exploiters, instead of turning their weapons against their own ruling classes as the socialists invited them to do, finds its material ground of explanation in the contradictory power relationship here referred to, and cannot be reduced to the question of "ideological clarity." By the same token, those who expect a radical change in this respect from the unification of *globalizing capital* and its *"global government"*—which would be combatively confronted by internationally united and fully class-conscious labor—are also bound to be disappointed. Capital is not going to oblige and do such a "favor" to labor for the simple reason that it cannot do so.

The hierarchical/conflictual articulation of capital remains the system's overall structuring principle, no matter how large, indeed how gigantic even, its constitutive units might be. This is due to the innermost nature of the system's decision-making processes. Given the irreconcilable structural antagonism between capital and labor, the latter must be categorically excluded from all meaningful decision making. This must be the case not only at the most comprehensive level but even at the constitutive "microcosms" in the particular productive units. For capital, as the alienated power of decision making, cannot possibly function without making its decisions absolutely unquestioned (by the labor force) in the particular workshops, or by the rival production complexes at the intermediary level, in a given country, or even at the most com prehensive scale (by the commanding personnel in charge of other internationally competing units). This is why capital's mode of decision making—in all known and feasible varieties of the capital system—must be a *top-down authoritarian* way of managing the various enterprises. Understandably, therefore, all talk about labor "sharing power" with, or "participating" in the decision-making processes of capital belongs to the realm of pure fiction, if not to the cynical camouflage of the real state of affairs.

This structurally determined inability to share power explains why the wide-ranging twentieth-century *monopolistic* developments had to assume the form of *takeovers*—"hostile" or "non-hostile" takeovers (ubiquitous today on a mind-boggling scale), but invariably takeovers, with one of the parties involved coming out on top, even when the ideological rationalization of the process is misrepresented as the "happy marriage of equals." The same inability explains, for our time even more significantly, the important fact that the ongoing globalization of capital produced and continues to produce giant transnational corporations, but not genuine multinationals, despite the much needed ideological convenience of the latter. No doubt in the future there will be many attempts to rectify this situation through the creation and operation of proper multinational companies. However, the underlying problem is bound to remain even in that circumstance. For the future "shared boardroom arrangements" of genuine multinationals are workable only *in the absence of significant conflicts of interest* among the particular national constituents of the multinationals in question. Once such conflicts arise, the former "harmonious collaborative arrangements" become unsustainable, and the overall decision-making process must revert to the customary authoritarian top-down variety, under the overpowering weight of the strongest member. For this problem is inseparable from the relationship of the particular national capitals to *their own labor force*, which remains always structurally antagonistic/conflictual.

Accordingly, in a situation of major conflict no particular national capital can afford—or permit—to become disadvantaged by decisions that would favor a rival national labor force, and by implication its own rival national capital-antagonist. The wishfully projected "world government" under the rule of capital would become feasible only if a workable solution could be found to this problem. But no government, and least of all a "world government," is feasible without a well-established and efficiently functioning material basis. The idea of a viable world government implies as its necessary material base the elimination of all significant material antagonisms from the global constitution of the capital system, and thereby the harmonious management of social metabolic reproduction by *one* uncontested global monopoly, embracing *all facets* of societal reproduction with the happy cooperation of the global labor force—a veritable contradiction in terms. Without this material base, it would require the totally authoritarian and, whenever necessary, extreme violent rule of the whole world by one hegemonic imperialist country on a permanent basis: an equally absurd and unsustainable way of running the world order. Only a socialist mode of social metabolic reproduction can offer a genuine alternative to these nightmare solutions.

Another vital objective determination we have to face, however uncomfortable it might be, concerns the nature of the political sphere and the parties within it. For the centralization of labor's sectionality—a sectionality which its political parties were expected to remedy—was due to a large extent to the necessary mode of operation of the political parties themselves, in their unavoidable opposition to their *political* adversary within the capitalist state representing the overall political command structure of capital. Thus all of labor's political parties, including the Leninist, had to appropriate for themselves the comprehensive political dimension, so as to be able to mirror in their own mode of articulation the underlying political structure (the bureaucratized capitalist state) to which they were subjected. What was problematical in all this was that the politically necessary and successful mirroring of the adversary's political structuring principle could not bring with it the practicable vision of an *alternative* way of controlling the system. Labor's political parties could not elaborate a viable alternative because they were centered in their negating function exclusively on the adversary's *political dimension*, remaining thereby utterly *dependent on the object of their negation*.

The vital missing dimension, which political parties as such cannot supply, was capital not as *political command* (that aspect was undoubtedly addressed) but as the *social metabolic regulator of the material reproduction process*, which ultimately determines also the political dimension, but much more than that besides. This unique correlation in the capital system between the political and the material reproductive dimension is what explains why we witness periodic moves, at times of major socioeconomic and political crises, from the parliamentary democratic articulation of politics to its extreme authoritarian varieties. These shifts take place as they are required or permitted by social metabolic processes in turmoil. And the political framework regulated by the *formal democratic rules of adversariality* is restored in due course, on capital's newly reconstituted and consolidated social metabolic ground.

Since capital is *actually* in control of all vital aspects of the social metabolism, it can afford to define the separately constituted sphere of political legitimation as a strictly *formal* matter, thereby *a priori* excluding the possibility of being legitimately challenged in its *substantive* sphere of socioeconomic reproductive operation. Conforming to such determinations, labor as the antagonist of actually existing capital can only condemn itself to permanent impotence. The postcapitalist historical experience tells a very sad cautionary tale in this respect, regarding its way of misdiagnosing and tackling the fundamental problems of the negated social order.

The capital system is made up from incorrigibly *centrifugal* (conflicting/adversarial) constituents, complemented as their *cohesive* dimension under capitalism not only by the unceremoniously overruling power of the "invisible hand," but also by the legal and political functions of the modern state. The failure of post-capitalist societies was that they tried to counter the centrifugal structuring determination of the inherited system by *superimposing* on its particular adversarial constituents the *extreme centralized command structure* of an authoritarian political state. This they did in place of addressing the crucial problem of how to *remedy*—through internal restructuring and the institution of *substantive democratic control*—the adversarial character and the concomitant centrifugal mode of functioning of the particular reproductive and distributive units. The removal of the private capitalist personifications of capital therefore could not fulfill its role even as the first step on the road of the promised socialist transformation. For the adversarial and centrifugal nature of the negated system was in fact retained through the superimposition of centralized political control at the expense of labor. Indeed, the social metabolic system was rendered more uncontrollable than ever before as a result of the failure to productively replace the "invisible hand" of the old reproductive order by the voluntarist authoritarianism of the "visible" new personifications of post-capitalist capital.

In contrast to the development of so-called actually existing socialism, what is required as the vital condition of success is the progressive reacquisition of the alienated powers of political—and not only political—decision making in the transition toward a genuine socialist society. Without the reacquisition of these powers neither the new mode of political control of society as a whole is conceivable, nor indeed the *non-adversarial* and thereby *cohesive* and *plannable* everyday operation of the particular productive and distributive units by their self-managing associated producers.

*The reconstitution of the unity of the material reproductive and the political sphere is the essential defining characteristic of the socialist mode of social metabolic control.* Creating the necessary mediations toward it cannot be left to some faraway future. This is where the defensive articulation and sectional centralization of the socialist movement in the twentieth century demonstrates its historical anachronism and untenability. Confining the comprehensive dimension of the radical hegemonic alternative to capital's mode of social metabolic control to the political sphere can never produce a successful outcome. However, as things stand today, the failure to address the vital social metabolic dimension of the system remains characteristic of labor's organized political embodiments. This is what represents the greatest historical challenge for the future.

### 3.4

The possibility of meeting this challenge by a radically rearticulated socialist movement is indicated by four major considerations.

The first is a negative one. It arises from the constantly aggravated contradictions of the existing order that underline the vacuity of the apologetic projections of its absolute permanence. For destructiveness can be stretched very far, as we know only too well from our constantly worsening conditions of existence, but not forever. Ongoing globalization is hailed by the defenders of the system as the solution to its problems. In reality, however, it sets into motion forces that put into relief not only the system's uncontrollability by rational design but simultaneously also its own inability to fulfill its controlling functions as the condition of its existence and legitimacy.

The second consideration indicates the possibility—but only the possibility—of a positive turn of events. Nevertheless, this possibility is very real because the capital/labor relation is not a *symmetrical* one. That means in the most important respect that while capital's dependency on labor is *absolute*—in that capital is absolutely nothing without labor, which it must permanently exploit—labor's dependency on capital is *relative, historically created and historically surmountable*. In other words, labor is not condemned to remain permanently locked into capital's vicious circle.

The third consideration is equally important. It concerns a major historical change in the confrontation between capital and labor, bringing with it the necessity to look for a very different way of asserting the vital interests of the "freely associated producers." This is in sharp contrast to the reformist past that had brought the movement to a dead end, liquidating at the same time even the most limited concessions squeezed out of capital in the past. Thus, for the first time in history, it has become quite untenable to maintain the mystifying gap between *immediate aims* and *overall strategic objectives*—which made the pursuit of the reformist blind alley so dominant in the labor movement. As a result, the question of *real control of an alternative social metabolic order* has appeared on the historical agenda, no matter how unfavorable the conditions of its realization for the time being.

And finally, as the necessary corollary of the last point, the question of *substantive equality* has also surfaced, in contrast to the *formal* equality and the most pronounced *substantive hierarchical inequality* of capital's decision-making processes as well as the way in which they were mirrored and reproduced in the failed post-capitalist historical experience. For the socialist alternative mode of controlling a *non-adversarial* and genuinely *plannable* social metabolic order—an absolute must for the future—is quite inconceivable without substantive equality as its structuring and regulating principle.

# 4. CONCLUSION

Following in Marx's footsteps, Rosa Luxemburg expressed in a striking way the dilemma we have to face: *"socialism or barbarism."* When Marx first formulated his early version of this idea, he situated it within the ultimate historical horizon of the contradictions then unfolding. In his view these contradictions were bound to confront the individuals sometime in the indeterminate future with the imperative to make the right choices about the social order to adopt, so as to save their very existence.

By the time Rosa Luxemburg talked about the stark alternative, the second historical phase of imperialism was in full swing, causing on a vast scale the kind of destruction that was quite unimaginable at an earlier stage of development. But the timescale of how long the capital system could continue to assert itself in the form of its "productive destruction" and "destructive production," was still indeterminate in Rosa Luxemburg's lifetime. For no single power—not even all of them put together—were capable of destroying humankind at the time with their devastating conflicts.

Today the situation is qualitatively different, and for that reason Rosa Luxemburg's sentence has acquired a dramatic urgency. There are no escape routes for workable conciliatory evasions. Yet, even if it can be asserted with certainty that the historical phase of global hegemonic imperialism, too, must fail, because it is incapable of resolving or postponing forever the system's explosive contradictions, this can promise no solution for the future. Many of the problems we have to confront—from chronic structural unemployment to the major international economic and political/military conflicts indicated above, as well as to the ever more widespread ecological destruction in evidence everywhere—require concerted action in the very near future. The timescale of such action may be measured perhaps in a few decades, but certainly not in centuries. We are running out of time. Thus, only a radical alternative to the established mode of controlling social metabolic reproduction can offer a way out of capital's structural crisis.

Those who talk about the "third way" as the solution to our dilemma, asserting that there can be no room for the revival of a radical mass movement, either want to deceive us by cynically calling their slavish acceptance of the ruling order "the third way," or fail to realize the gravity of the situation, putting their faith in a wishfully non-conflictual positive outcome that has been promised for nearly a century but never approximated even by one inch. The uncomfortable truth of the matter is that if there is no future for a radical mass movement in our time, there can be no future for humanity itself.

If I had to modify Rosa Luxemburg's dramatic words, in relation to the dangers we now face, I would add to "socialism or barbarism" this qualification: "barbarism if we are lucky." For the *extermination of humanity* is the ultimate concomitant of capital's destructive course of development. And the world of that third possibility, beyond the alternatives of "socialism or barbarism," would be fit only for cockroaches, which are said to be able to endure lethally high levels of nuclear radiation. This is the only rational meaning of *capital's third way*.

The now fully operative third and potentially deadliest phase of global hegemonic imperialism, corresponding to the profound structural crisis of the capital system as a whole on the political and military plane, leaves us no room for comfort or cause for self-assurance. Instead, it casts the darkest possible shadow on the future, in case the historical challenges facing the socialist movement fail to be successfully met in the time still within our reach. This is why the century in front of us is bound to be the century of "socialism or barbarism."

# PART II

## MARXISM, THE CAPITAL SYSTEM, AND SOCIAL REVOLUTION

### AN INTERVIEW

*The following interview was given to the quarterly journal Naghd (Critique) on June 2, 1998 (no. 25, Spring 1999). The author gratefully acknowldeges the first English publication in Science and Society, 63:3 (Fall 1999).*

**NAGHD: In your opinion which of the Marxian models can explain the capitalist crises of the modern age?**
**1. The model of reproduction of total social capital?**
**2. The model of overproduction?**
**3. The tendency for the profit rate to fall?**
**4. Or can we combine all these models into one?**

**ISTVÁN MÉSZÁROS:** Yes, fundamentally you can combine them. But what takes precedence is after all a global view of capital. It is quite ironical that people have been recently discovering that we live in a world of "globalization." This was always self-evident to Marx, and I discussed it in the same way in my Isaac Deutscher Memorial Lecture ("The Necessity of Social Control," 1971; this lecture is now reprinted in Part IV of *Beyond Capital*). There I talk at length about "globalization"—not using that word, but the crucial equivalent categories of "total social capital" and the "totality of labor." The conceptual framework in which you can make sense of the capital system can only be a global one. Capital has absolutely no way of restraining itself, nor can you find in the world a counterforce that could restrain it without radically overcoming the capital system as such. So capital had to run its course and logic of development: it had to embrace the totality of the planet. That was always implicit in Marx.

The other things you have mentioned, like the "declining rate of profit," etc. are in a way subsidiary to the globally expansionary logic of capital, so that you can incorporate all in the global vision. The capital system has a multiplicity of particular constituents, full of contradictions. You have a plurality of capitals, both nationally confronting one another as well as internal to any national community. In fact the plurality of capitals within particular national communities constitutes the theoretical basis of liberalism, deluding itself that it is the champion of Liberty writ large. Capital is not a homogeneous entity. This carries with it great complications to the whole question of "globalization." The way it is customarily presented, "globalization" is a complete fantasy, suggesting that we are all going to live under a capitalistic "global government," unproblematically obeying the rules of this unified global government. That is quite inconceivable. There can be no way of bringing the capital system under one big monopoly that would provide the material basis of such a "global government." In reality, we have a multiplicity of divisions and contradictions, and "total social capital" is the comprehensive category that incorporates the plurality of capitals, with all their contradictions.

Now, if you look at the other side, also the "totality of labor" can never be considered a homogeneous entity for as long as the capital system survives. There are, of necessity, so many contradictions that you find under the given historical conditions among sections of labor, opposing and fighting one another, competing against one another, rather than simply confronting particular sections of capital. This is one of the tragedies of our predicament today. And it cannot be simply wished out of existence. For, as Marx had put it a long time ago:

Competition separates individuals from one another, not only the bourgeois but still more the workers, in spite of the fact that it brings them together. Hence every organized power standing over against these isolated individuals, who live in conditions daily reproducing this isolation, can only be overcome after long struggles. To demand the opposite would be tantamount to demanding that competition should not exist in this definite epoch of history, or that the individuals should banish from their minds conditions over which in their isolation they have no control.

These divisions and contradictions remain with us and ultimately they are all to be explained by the nature and functioning of the capital system itself. It is an insuperably contradictory system based on social antagonism. It is an adversarial system, based on the structural domination of labor by capital. So there are of necessity all kinds of sectional divisions.

But we must also bear in mind that we are talking about a dynamically unfolding system. The dynamically unfolding tendency of the global capital system cannot help being a totally and inextricably intertwined, and at the same time deeply contradictory, system. This is why all those other models you have mentioned can be subsumed under the intrinsic determinations of globally unfolding "total social capital" and the corresponding "totality of labor." This general framework has its own logic, in the sense of inexorably unfolding in accordance with its intrinsic structural determinations and limitations. There are some absolute—historically untranscendable—limitations to this system. I have tried to spell these out in Chapter 5 of *Beyond Capital* entitled "The Activation of Capital's Absolute Limits."

**N: What is the validity of criticism regarding Marx's theory of the "conversion of value to price" and the Marxian response to that criticism?**

**IM:** Well, I think it may be too technical to go into the details. You know the way in which modern economic theory has questioned these points. But I don't think that we can make much of it, in that the market system under which we operate makes it necessary to provide this conversion. This takes us back to the question of the "labor theory of value." The foundation of the Marxian conceptual framework is the labor theory of value, concerning the way in which "surplus value" is generated and appropriated under the rule of capital. Since under our present conditions of socioeconomic reproduction in most countries we have a market framework in which the plurality of capitals that I mentioned earlier must adjust itself. You mentioned the "profit rate" which is also in the process of constant adjustment. But this adjustment cannot take place without the intermediary of conversion.

If (and where) capital had a straightforward political way of controlling the system's expanded reproduction, there would be (and there was) no need for the intermediary of genuine conversion. The process could be more or less arbitrarily settled on the basis of political decisions, as it actually happened under the Soviet-type capital system. In other words, we are again concerned with a subsidiary element of the overall theory. It is a matter of secondary importance whether surplus labor is appropriated politically or economically. What is of primary importance is that under all conceivable varieties of the capital system surplus labor must be appropriated by a separate body superimposed on, and structurally dominating, labor. Here, as you can see, the fundamental category is "surplus labor," and not "surplus value," as people often erroneously assume. "Surplus value" and the specific forms of its appropriation and realization are absolutely essential under *capitalism*. But the capital system embraces much more than its capitalist variety. There have been—and indeed even today there are still in existence—forms of the capital system that cannot be simply described as capitalist.

You know that many people have tried to characterize the now defunct Soviet system as "state capitalist." I do not think that such characterization makes any sense at all. The Soviet system was not "state capitalist"; it was "*post-capitalist.*" Nevertheless, this system also operated on the basis of the appropriation of surplus *labor* by a separate body, structurally dominating labor and operating the *political extraction of surplus labor*. In other words, the Soviet labor force was not in control of the regulation and allocation of its own surplus labor, which in that system did not have to be converted into surplus value. The Soviet-type system was a historically specific form of the capital system in which the appropriation of surplus labor had to be *politically controlled*.

That is what has come to an end in the former Soviet Union, but by no means everywhere. In the Chinese system you still find the predominance of the political control of surplus labor extraction. Although many people talk about the "market framework of the Chinese system," in reality—when you consider the totality of China's social metabolic reproduction—the market is very much subsidiary to it. So, primarily, in the Chinese system the political appropriation of surplus labor is still going on, and indeed on a massive scale. In this sense, when you look at the problem of conversion from the angle of "surplus labor," rather than "surplus value"—which must be present in a *particular* variety of the capital system—then you find that in the capitalist variety (based on surplus value) it is essential to operate with the intermediary of conversion whose particular details are historically contingent. They also depend on the historic phases of capitalist developments. Thus the more advanced monopolistic phases of capitalist development must obviously operate in a significantly different way the conversion of surplus value into prices, as compared to a much earlier phase of development known to Marx.

**N: Under what conditions would the "Theory of Value" not have any validity? Are such conditions technological, economic or related to the human factor?**

**IM:** The "labor theory of value" can cease to operate only as a result of a radical socialist transformation. That is the first thing to stress. In order to do away with the labor theory of value, you have to do away with the extraction and allocation of surplus labor by an external body of any sort, be that political or economic. But to do away with it, you have to change the whole system altogether. In other words, we can only speak about socialism when the people are in control of their own activity and of the allocation of its fruits to their own ends. This means the self-activity and self-control of society by the "associated producers," as Marx had put it. Naturally, the "associated producers" cannot control their activity and its objectives unless they also control the allocation of the socially produced surplus. It is therefore inconceivable to institute socialism if a separate body remains in control of the extraction and appropriation of surplus labor. Under socialism the labor theory of value has absolutely no validity; there is no room for it.

Marx talks about the *"miserable foundation"* under which in the capital system the perverse extraction of surplus labor must be the regulator of the social reproduction process. To be sure, in every society you need a way of dealing with the problem of how to allocate the resources. For what is the meaning of "economy"? It is fundamentally a rational way of *economizing*. We do not have infinite resources to squander at will, as it happens—to our peril—under the capital system. We do not have an infinite amount of anything, whether you think of material resources or of human energy, at any particular time. Thus we need a rational regulation of the social reproduction process. The important thing is the viability of the social reproduction process on a long-term basis, rather than within the irresponsibly myopic and thoroughly unsustainable confines of the capital system. This is why it is necessary to reorient societal interchange from the tyranny of surplus value and from the expropriation of the surplus labor of the producers by a separate body to a qualitatively different one. In the latter, in which the "associated producers" are in control of both the production and the allocation of their products, there is absolutely no room for surplus value to impose itself upon the social individuals. That is to say, there is no room for the imperatives of capital and capital accumulation.

This is because capital is not simply a material entity. We must think of capital as a historically determinate way of controlling social metabolic reproduction. That is the fundamental meaning of capital. It penetrates everywhere. Of course, capital is also a material entity; gold, banking, price mechanisms, market mechanisms, etc. But well beyond that, capital also penetrates in the world of art, in the world of religion and the churches, running society's cultural institutions. You cannot think of anything in contemporary life that is not controlled by capital in that sense under the present circumstances. That is why the "labor theory of value" is valid for the historical period when capital is all-embracing, when the regulation process itself is fundamentally irrational.

And this is by no means the end of the story. It is further complicated by the fact that in the difficult historical period of transition from the rule of capital to a very different system the labor theory of value and the law of value function in a very imperfect way. This is one of the reasons why the Soviet-type capital system was doomed. It was a transitional system that could go either in one direction, towards a socialist transformation of society, which it did not do; or it had to implode and embark on the road of capitalist restoration sooner or later. This is what we have witnessed, because at a certain point in time the Soviet system was, so to speak, "falling between two stools." It had no way of regulating the economy by some sort of economic mechanism like the market, the price system, and so on. Therefore it could not have the kind of labor-disciplining force that we have under the capitalist market system.

In our society so many things are settled automatically by market forces; labor is ruthlessly subjected to the prevailing conditioning tyranny of the market. The crucial question in this regard is, precisely, the labor market. If you look back to the time when the Soviet system under Gorbachev collapsed, you will see that the system's demise coincided with the ill-conceived and futile attempt to introduce into it the labor market. That was the end of the much-advertised perestroika. For the labor market can work properly only under capitalist conditions. That is where the law of value prevailed—not partially or marginally, but in principle as a matter of course—in the "expanded reproduction of capital." There were all kinds of limits beyond the capitalist world—namely the global framework—under which also the Soviet system had to operate. Under the conditions of twentieth century development many things that could work in the past within the framework of the economically regulated extraction of surplus labor have become most problematical. Today the imperfections of the market and the far from unproblematical operation of the law of value are clearly in evidence also in our system in the advanced capitalist countries of the West. The ever-greater role assumed by the state—without which the capital system could not survive today in our societies—puts very serious constraints on the law of value in our system. Here we are talking about potentially far-reaching limitations that are of course the system's self-contradictions.

It must be also added that it is one thing to *attempt* the full restoration of capitalism in the former Soviet Union, and quite another to succeed with it. Because *fifteen years* after Gorbachev had started the process of capitalist restoration one can only talk about *partial* successes, confined primarily to the mafia-ridden business circles of the major cities. The endemic and chronic crisis in Russia, strikingly manifest also in the form that many groups of workers—for instance, the miners—do not have even their miserable wages paid for several months, sometimes up to a year and a half, which is inconceivable in a proper capitalist framework where the fundamental regulator of surplus-labor extraction is economic and not political. This highlights a vital trend of twentieth century development. It is a fact of world-historical significance that the capital system could not complete itself in the twentieth century in the form of its *capitalist variety*, based on the economic regulation of surplus-labor extraction. So much so, that today approximately one-half of the world's population—from China to India and to important areas of Africa, South East Asia and Latin America—do not belong to the world of capitalism proper, but live under some hybrid variety of the capital system, either due to chronically underdeveloped conditions, or to massive state involvement in regulating the socioeconomic metabolism, or indeed to a combination of the two. The endemic crisis in Russia—which may well end in total destabilization and potential explosion—can only be explained in this context. Understandably, the true significance of this world-historical fact—i.e. of the failure of capitalism to successfully impose itself everywhere, despite all self-complacent talk about "globalization"—is bound to take some time to sink in, given the mythologies of the past and the now predominant triumphalism. However, this cannot diminish the significance of the fact itself and of its far-reaching implications for the future that must arise from the deepening structural crisis of the capital system.

**N: Where is the proletariat today and what role does it play in social change? Where can we find the agency for social change today?**

IM: I think what you are really asking concerns the social agency of transformation. For that is what the word "proletariat" summed up at the time of Marx. At that time, the word often meant the industrial proletariat. The industrial working classes are on the whole manual workers, from mining to various branches of industrial production. To confine the social agency of change to manual workers was obviously not Marx's own position. Marx was very far from thinking that the concept of "manual workers" would provide an adequate framework of explanation of what is required for radical social change. You must recall that he was talking about how through the polarization of society ever greater numbers of people are "proletarianized." So, it is the process of proletarianization—inseparable from the global unfolding of the capital system—that defines and ultimately settles the issue. That is to say, the question is how the overwhelming majority of individuals fall into a condition whereby they lose all possibilities of control of their lives, and in that sense they become proletarianized. Thus, again, everything comes down to the question of "who is in control" of the social reproduction process when the overwhelming majority of individuals are "proletarianized" and degraded to the condition of utter powerlessness, as the most wretched members of society—the "proletarians"—were at an earlier phase of development.

There are degrees and possibilities of control, up to a certain point in capital's history, which means that some sections of the population are more in control than others. In fact, Marx in one of the chapters of *Capital* was describing the capitalist enterprise as almost a military operation in which you have officers and sergeants, and the foremen like sergeants are overseeing and regulating the direct labor force on the authority of capital. Ultimately all of the control processes are under the authority of capital, but with certain leverages and possibilities of limited autonomy assigned to the particular overseeing sections. Now, when you talk about advancing "proletarianization," it implies a leveling down and the negation of even the most limited autonomy some groups of people formerly enjoyed in the labor process.

Just think of the once sharply stressed distinction between "white-collar" and "blue-collar" workers. As you know, the propagandists of the capital system who dominate the cultural and intellectual processes like to use the distinction between the two as yet another refutation of Marx, arguing that in our societies blue-collar manual work altogether disappears, and the white-collar workers, who are supposed to enjoy a much greater job security (which happens to be a complete fiction), are elevated into the "middle classes" (another fiction). Well,

I would say even about the postulated disappearance of blue-collar work: hold on, not so fast! For if you look around the world and focus on the crucial category of the "totality of labor," you find that the overwhelming majority of labor still remains what you might describe as "blue-collar." In this respect it is enough to think of the hundreds of millions of blue-collar workers in India, for instance.

**N: Can I add something to it? Is Marx's distinction between productive and non-productive labor sufficient?**

**IM:** Well, it is sufficient in the sense that you can make that distinction. When you consider the overall reproduction process, you find that certain constituents of the overall reproduction process are becoming more and more parasitic. Think of the ever-rising administration costs and insurance costs in this regard. The most extreme form of parasitism in our contemporary reproduction process is, of course, the financial sector, constantly engaged in global speculation, with very severe—and potentially extremely grave—repercussions on the production process properly so called. The dangerous parasitism of the speculative international financial sector  which, to add insult to injury, continues to be glorified under the propagandist slogan of unavoidable and universally beneficial "globalization"— has an important bearing on the future prospects of social transformation. This takes us back to the vital question of the social agency of change. What decides the matter is not the historically changing relationship between "blue-collar" and "white-collar" workers, but the socially untranscendable fundamental confrontation between capital and labor. This is not confined to this or that particular section of labor but embraces the totality of labor as the antagonist of capital. In other words, labor as the antagonist of capital—i.e. of globally self-asserting "total social capital," can only be the "totality of labor," on a global scale—subsumes under itself all sections and varieties of labor, whatever their socioeconomic configuration at the present stage of history. We have witnessed what is going on in our societies, in the so-called advanced capitalist societies of the West. As it happened and continues to happen, vast numbers of white-collar workers were and are ruthlessly ejected from the labor process. Indeed, hundreds of thousands of them in every major country.

Look at this question in the United States. Once upon a time the white-collar workers had some sort of job security, accompanied by a relative little autonomy for their kind of activity. All this is now disappearing, going out of the window. Here computerized "advanced machinery" and the question of technology very much enter the picture. But even in this context technology always takes the secondary place to the imperative of capital accumulation. That is what ultimately decides the issue, using the "inevitable progress of technology" as its alibi for crushing human lives on a massive scale. So, we have the proletarianization of a labor force that was once upon a time more secure. This is an ongoing process. Unemployment is endemic and ubiquitous; you cannot find a single country today that does not have it to an increasing degree. I mentioned in my Introduction to the Farsi edition of *Beyond Capital* that in India there are *three hundred and thirty-six million* people (336,000,000!) on the unemployment registers; and you can imagine how many more millions are not registered at all. This is the predicament of humanity today. Just look around, what is happening in Latin America, the growing unemployment in Africa, and even in Japan: not so many years ago hailed as the "miracle" country. Now every month I read in Japanese publications about new record levels of unemployment. In fact, Japan today has a considerably higher rate of unemployment than the United States. What an irony. For not so long ago the Japanese way of dealing with these problems used to be considered the ideal solution.

The cancerous growth of unemployment is affecting every single country today, including those that did not have it in the past. Take Hungary, for instance. Now it has an unemployment rate higher than the very high rate in Germany. Here you can see the big difference between the capitalist and the Soviet type post-capitalist system. There was no unemployment in the Soviet-type countries in the past. There were various forms of underemployment, but no unemployment. Now in Hungary unemployment is equivalent to something much higher than we have not only in Germany but also in Britain and in Italy. Look at what is happening in Russia. Russia once did not experience unemployment, and now its unemployment rate is massive. And, as mentioned earlier, even if you are employed in Russia, like the miners, you may not receive your wages for months. You have to bear in mind all the time that we are talking about a dynamic process of unfolding and transformation. This process threatens humanity with devastation, and the social agency that can do something about it—indeed the only feasible agency capable of instituting an *alternative* way of controlling the social metabolism—is labor. Not particular sections of labor, but the totality of labor as the *irreconcilable antagonist of capital*.

**N: Before I start asking about the objective possibility/the real possibility of socialism, I would like to ask about Marx. What aspects of Marx's theory are vulnerable or need to be renewed? Which parts do you think need it? Methodology, sociology, historical or economic theory?**

**IM:** The Marxian framework is always in need of renewal. Marx was writing in the middle of the nineteenth century and died in 1883. Things have changed immeasurably since that time. The tendencies of transformation which we have witnessed in the recent past, with their roots going back to the first few decades of our century, are of such a character that Marx could not even dream about them. Above all, this concerns the way in which the capital system could adjust and renew itself, so as to postpone the unfolding and maturation of its antagonistic contradictions. Marx was not in a situation in which he could have assessed the various modalities and the ultimate limitations of state intervention in prolonging the lifespan of the capital system. A key figure in twentieth century economic development is John Maynard Keynes. Keynes' fundamental aim was precisely to save the system through the injection of massive state funds for the benefit of private capitalist enterprise, so as to regulate on a permanent basis within the framework of undisturbed capital accumulation the overall reproduction process.

Now, more recently "monetarism" and "neo-liberalism" have pushed Keynes aside and indulged in the fantasy of doing away with state intervention altogether, envisaging the "rolling back the boundaries of the state" in a most absurd way. Naturally, in reality nothing could correspond to such self-serving fantasies. In fact the role of the state in the contemporary capitalist system is greater than ever before, including the time of the postwar two and a half decades of Keynesian developments in the capitalistically most advanced countries. This kind of development is totally new as compared to Marx's lifetime.

Adding even more to the complications, is what happened in the former Soviet Union and in general to the Soviet-type system. When you have a revolution that wants to be socialist, with the objective of bringing about a socialist transformation of society, that is one thing. But when you look at the type of society that came out of it, you must say that it is something quite different. Because the rule of capital continued—even if in a very different way—in the Soviet-type post-capitalist system. Looking at it more closely, we find an important connection with Marx. For Marx talks about the "personifications of capital," which is a very important category. Marx uses this category when he talks about the private capitalists, since there was no other form visible in his lifetime. But he perceives, with great insight, that what truly defines the commanding personnel of the capital system is that they are *personifications of capital*. They have to operate under the objective imperatives of capital as such.

The ideologists and propagandists of capitalism like to perpetuate the mythology of the "enlightened capitalist" and the "benevolent caring capitalist" who are bound to take very good care of the workers as the general rule, referring to those who behave differently as "the unacceptable face of capitalism," to use former Conservative British Prime Minister Edward Heath's expression. This is a grotesque fantasy, even when it is not voiced with complete cynicism. For all capitalists have to submit to the objective imperatives emanating from the unalterable logic of capital expansion. If they do not do so, they will quickly cease to be capitalists, unceremoniously ejected from the overall reproduction process as viable commanding personnel by the selfsame logic. It is inconceivable for the capitalists to function on the basis of being the helpers of working class aspirations. That would be a contradiction in terms, given the necessary structural domination of labor by capital in all conceivable varieties of the capital system.

That takes us back to the question of the "personifications of capital" as the connecting link with Marx's vision. For the "personifications of capital" must obey and impose on the workers the objective imperatives emanating from the logic of capital, according to the changing socio-historical circumstances. And that is highly relevant to understanding the way in which you can have the variety of different "personifications of capital" which we have witnessed in the twentieth-century. Marx knew only one form in which capital was personified: the private capitalist, whether a single individual or combination of shareholders. But we have seen several different forms, and may still see some new and quite unexpected permutations in the future, as the structural crisis of the global capital system unfolds.

One of the principal reasons why I wrote *Beyond Capital* was precisely to consider the future. We must focus on the future with critical eyes in order to be active participants in the historical process, fully aware of and concerned about the fateful implications of capital's destructive power at the present stage of history. Capital has been with us for a very long time in one form or another; indeed in some of its more limited forms for thousands of years. Nevertheless, only in the last three to four hundred years in the form of capitalism which could fully work out the self-expansionary logic of capital, no matter how devastating the consequences for the very survival of humanity. This is what must be put in perspective. When we are thinking about the future, in the light of our painful historical experience we cannot imagine a situation in which the overthrow of capitalism—in terms of which in the past we used to think about the socialist revolution—solves the grave problems confronting us. For capital is ubiquitous; it is deeply embedded in every single area of our social life. Consequently, if we are to have any success at all, capital must be eradicated from everywhere through a laborious process of profound social transformation. The aspirations of socialist change on a lasting basis must be related to that, with all its difficulties. It is necessary to guard constantly against the potential personifications of capital imposing themselves on the objectives of future socialist revolutions. Our perspective must orient itself toward devising and successfully asserting the necessary safeguards against the reappearance of the personifications of capital, in whatever new form.

The Marxian framework must be constantly renewed in that sense, so as to be able to cope with the bewildering twists and turns of "the cunning of history." There is no area of theoretical activity—and Marx would be the first to agree to this proposition; in fact he did so explicitly—which could escape the need for thoroughly renewing itself with every major historical change. And the fact is that from Marx's lifetime to our present conditions there has been a massive historical change.

Just to mention one more important consideration in conclusion to this question, Marx was to some extent already aware of the "ecological problem," i.e. the problems of ecology under the rule of capital and the dangers implicit in it for human survival. In fact he was the first to conceptualize it. He talked about pollution, and he insisted that the logic of capital—which must pursue profit, in accordance with the dynamic of self-expansion and capital accumulation—cannot have any consideration for human values and even for human survival. The elements of this discourse you can find in Marx. (His remarks on the subject are discussed in the 1971 lecture on *The Necessity of Social Control* mentioned earlier.)

What you cannot find in Marx, of course, is an account of the utmost gravity of the situation facing us. For us the threat to human survival is a matter of *immediacy*. We can easily destroy humanity today. The means and weapons are already at our disposal for the total destruction of humanity. Nothing of the kind was on the horizon in Marx's lifetime. The underlying destructive imperatives can only be explained in terms of the mad logic capital applies to the question of *economy*. As I stressed earlier, the true meaning of economy in the human situation cannot be other than *economizing* on a long-term basis. Today we find the exact opposite. The way in which the capital system operates makes a mockery of the necessity of economizing. Indeed, it pursues everywhere with utmost irresponsibility the opposite of economy: total *wastefulness*. It is this profit-seeking wastefulness that directly endangers the very survival of humanity, presenting us with the challenge of doing something about it as a matter of great *urgency*. This was unthinkable under the conditions when Marx had to write, although you can *project* the words on pollution which he wrote in his critique of Feuerbach's ahistorical assessment of nature, amounting to an idealization of nature taken completely out of its social context and totally ignoring the impact on nature necessarily exercised by capital's labor process. You can find Marx's critical remarks in *The German Ideology*, but obviously not a full development of this complex of problems as they confront us in their immediacy and urgency.

In March 1998 we celebrated the 150th anniversary of *The Communist Manifesto*. The question is: has humanity got another 150 years to go? Certainly not if the capital system survives! What we have to face is either total catastrophe, due to the capital system's monstrous wastefulness, or humanity must find a radically different way of regulating its social metabolism!

**N: How do you describe the objective/real possibility of socialism?**

**IM:** For the moment this is a very difficult question, because of what has happened in the recent past and in some ways is still happening. What we have to bear in mind is that the great historical challenge for present and future generations is to move from one type of social metabolic order to a radically different one. It cannot be stressed enough what an immense and difficult historic task this is. It never had to be faced in the past with the dramatic urgency that is inescapable today.

The social order of capital that we are all familiar with has culminated in an all-embracing and dominating system in the last three to four hundred years. In the twentieth century it has also succeeded in suffocating, undermining or corrupting every major political effort aimed at going against and beyond it. But it would be a great illusion to assume that this means the end of socialism. This is how in the last few years, neo-liberal propaganda tried to describe what has happened, triumphalistically shouting "We have done away with socialism once and for all." Mrs. Thatcher, during her decade as Prime Minister of Britain, boasted that she had "seen off socialism for good." She was talking about the working class movement, groups of workers and trade unionists, especially the miners. At the time there was a miners' strike that has been defeated by the combined efforts of the capitalist state and the Labour Party leadership under Neal Kinnock. Mrs. Thatcher characterized the miners as "the enemy within." Despite its liberal pretenses her side has no fear of, nor reservations about, talking of you and of all those who maintain their aspirations for the establishment of a socialist order as "the enemy" and "the enemy within."

At the present time, if you look around the world you find that capital has the upper hand everywhere. But is it able to solve the grave problems constantly created by the functioning of its own mode of social metabolic reproduction? Far from it. On the contrary, given its insuperable antagonistic contradictions, capital is unable to address these problems. Instead, it continues to generate them on an ever-increasing scale. This is what keeps on the historical agenda the question of socialism, despite even the most massive and concerted efforts aimed at doing away with it. Capital's success consists only in *postponing* the time when it becomes an unavoidable necessity to confront the grave problems of its system, which still continue to accumulate. There have been many social explosions in the past in response to the contradictions of the established social order, going back to 1848 and 1871, and in some ways to the French Revolution of 1789 and its aftermath. Yet the aspirations of people for a truly equitable social order have been frustrated until now, and on the whole even the most heroic attempts have been countered and repressed by the power of capital, in one way or in another. So many of the encountered problems remain perilously unsolved. What is in this sense quite untenable is precisely the kind of adversarial, antagonistic mode of social reproduction process that both continues to generate our grave problems and at the same time prevents their solution. For the adversarial structural determinations constitute an absolute necessity for the functioning and reproduction of the existing system, whatever the consequences might be. These determinations are ineradicable. Notwithstanding all triumphalism, they are not going to go away. The devastating consequences of such a structure will come back again and again. There can be only one kind of solution: the removal of the structural antagonism from our social metabolic reproduction. And that in its terms is conceivable only if the transformation embraces everything, from the smallest constitutive cells of our society to the largest monopolistic transnational corporations that continue to dominate our life.

Thus, although in a superficial sense capital is undoubtedly triumphant, in a much more fundamental sense it is in the gravest possible trouble. This may sound paradoxical. Yet, if you recognize the way in which capital can dominate the social reproduction process everywhere, you must also recognize that it is structurally incapable of resolving its problems and contradictions. Wherever you look you find that what appears to be—and is loudly advertised as—a rock-solid lasting solution, sooner or later crumbles into dust. For instance, just try to survey in your mind the ephemeral history of "economic miracles" we had in the postwar decades. What sort of "miracles" were they? We had the "German miracle" and the "Japanese miracle," followed by the Italian, Brazilian, etc. "miracles." As we may well remember, the latest of them was the most tendentiously advertised miracle of the "Asian tiger economies." And what happened to that "miracle"? Like all the others, it has evaporated, leaving its place to a severe crisis. Today you cannot find one single country in the world that is not facing some absolutely fundamental problems, including the recent calamities on the stock exchanges of Russia and several Eastern European countries. Well, if you now read the bourgeois newspapers, they are all in some sort of panic. Their headlines frighten even themselves as to what is really going on. I remember that at the time when the "Asian miracle" was at its peak, the notion of this pretended "miracle" was also used as an overwhelming disciplinary argument against the working classes of the Western capitalist countries. "Behave yourself! Accept the standard of living and the work practices of the kind which the workers in the Asian tiger economies do, or you will be in deep trouble!" A system which claims to have resolved all its problems in the "post-industrial" Western "advanced capitalist" countries, and then has to rely for its continued health on such an authoritarian blackmailing message, does not promise much for the future even in its own terms of reference. Again, in this respect there is, and there can only be, one viable and sustainable solution.

It is socialism: socialism in the sense which I mentioned earlier; i.e. the elimination of the now given adversarial/antagonistic framework in which one section of the population—a tiny minority—has to dominate the overwhelming majority as a matter of insurmountable structural determination. That is to say, a form of domination that totally expropriates for itself the power of decision making. Labor as the antagonist of capital has absolutely no power of decision making; not even in the most limited context. That is the vital and unavoidable question for the future. And in that sense, I am convinced that the chances for the revival of the socialist movement sooner or later are absolutely great and fundamental.

**N: The concept of "revolution" in your opinion?**

**IM:** Yes, the concept of revolution remains very important and valid if we define it as a profound ongoing revolutionary transformation of all facets of our social life. One should not take the concept of revolution to mean "one big push that settles everything once and for all," nourishing the illusion that after cutting off a few heads you have won. For Marx's use of the concept of revolution—clearly stated in many contexts—was "social revolution." He said that the big difference between past revolutions and a socialist "social revolution" was that the revolutions of the past were essentially political in character, which meant changing the ruling personnel of society, while leaving the overwhelming majority of the people in their position of structural subordination. This is also the context in which the question of the "personifications of capital" must be considered. It is relatively easy to break a smaller or greater number of heads during the "big push" to overturn something; and this usually happens in the political sphere. This is the sense in which the concept of "revolution" was defined even recently.

Now, we know from bitter experience that it did not work. To proceed in that way is not enough. So we have to go back to what

Marx was saying about the "social revolution." I must also emphasize that this concept of the social revolution was not originally Marx's own idea. It is a concept that emerged from *Babeuf* and his movement way back during the turbulent aftermath of the 1789 French Revolution. Babeuf was executed at that time, accused with his group of "conspiracy." In reality he was pressing for "a society of equals." The same concept reappeared in the 1830s and during the revolutions of 1848. In such times of revolutionary upheaval the idea of "social revolution" was in the foreground of the most progressive forces, and Marx very rightly embraced it.

In a radical social transformation—we are talking about a socialist revolution—the change cannot be confined to the ruling personnel and hence the revolution must be all-embracing and truly social. That means that the transformation and the new mode of controlling the social metabolism must penetrate into every segment of society. It is in that sense that the concept of revolution remains valid; indeed, in the light of our historical experience, more valid than ever before. A revolution, in this sense, not only eradicates but also implants. The eradication is as much a part of this process as what you put in the place of what has been eradicated. Marx says somewhere that the meaning of "radical" is "to grasp matters at their roots." That is the literal meaning of being radical, and it retains its validity in the social revolution in the just mentioned sense of eradicating and implanting.

So much of what is today firmly rooted has to be eradicated in the future through the laborious processes of an ongoing—if you like "permanent"—revolutionary transformation. But the terrain on which this is done cannot be left empty. You have to put in the place of what has been removed something capable of taking deep roots. Talking about the social order of capital, Marx uses the expression "an organic system." I quoted a passage where he talks about it in the Introduction to the Farsi edition of *Beyond Capital*. The capital system under which we live is an *organic system*. Every part of it supports and reinforces the others. It is this kind of *reciprocal support* of the parts that makes the problem of revolutionary transformation very complicated and difficult. If you want to replace capital's organic system you have to put in its place *another organic system* in which the parts support the whole because the parts also reciprocally support each other. This is how the new system becomes viable, capable of standing firm, growing, and successfully moving in the direction that secures the gratification of every member of society.

Clearly, then, "revolution" cannot simply be a question of "overthrowing." Anything that can be overthrown can only be a very partial aspect of the *social revolution*. The historically known varieties of *capitalism* can be overthrown—in some limited contexts it has already happened—but *capital* itself cannot be "overthrown." It has to be eradicated, in the sense described above, and something must be put in its place. Likewise, the *capitalist state* can be overthrown. However, once you have overthrown the capitalist state, you have not removed the problem itself, because the *state as such* cannot be overthrown. This is why Marx is talking about the "withering away of the state," which is a fundamentally different concept. Moreover, the thorniest of these problems concerning the task of revolutionary transformation is that *labor as such* cannot be "overthrown." How do you "overthrow" labor as—together with capital and the state—one of the three supporting pillars of the capital system? For labor is the basis of the reproduction of society.

In the last few decades there have been all kinds of fantasies that the "information revolution" has done away with labor for good, and we live happily ever after in the "post-industrial society." The idea of work becoming play has a respectable lineage, going back to Friedrich Schiller. However, its capital-apologetic recent renewals constitute a complete absurdity. You can abolish *wage labor* by decree. But that is very far from solving the problem of labor's emancipation, which is conceivable only as the *self*-emancipation of the associated producers. Human labor as productive activity always remains the absolute condition of the reproduction process. The natural substratum of the individuals' existence is nature itself that must be rationally and creatively *controlled* by productive activity—as opposed to being irresponsibly and destructively *dominated* by the irrational, wasteful and destructive imperatives of capital-expansion. The social metabolism involves the necessary interchange among individuals themselves and between the totality of individuals and recalcitrant nature. Even the original, non-apologetic idea of work as play in the eighteenth century was inseparable from the idealization of nature: the ignorance or denial of its necessary recalcitrance. But the recent capital-apologetic rejoinders defy all belief, given the overwhelming evidence of the wanton destruction of nature by capital that the proponents of such theories cynically ignore.

You must have read books and articles in the last two or three decades about the so-called post-industrial society. What does that mean? "Post-industrial"? For so long as humanity survives, it must be industrious. It has to work to reproduce itself. It has to create the conditions under which human life not only remains possible but also becomes richer in human fulfillment. And that is conceivable only through industry in the most profound sense of the term. We will always be industrial. The idea that the "information revolution" will render all industrial work completely superfluous will never be more than a self-serving propagandist fantasy.

Characteristically, at the same time that the champions of capital-apologetics were talking about the "post-industrial" paradise, they were also approvingly talking about transferring the "smoke-stack industries" to India, or to China, to the Philippines, or to Latin America. So the "smoke-stack industries" have to be removed from the "advanced capitalist" West! But where do the "captains of industry" put the poisonous smoke-stacks of Union Carbide? They are transferred to Bhopal in India, with catastrophic consequences, killing several thousand people and blinding and injuring countless thousands more. Does that make society "post-industrial"? Far from it. Such "transfers of technology" only mean that the capitalist West sends its dirty linen to some "underdeveloped" part of the world—the so-called Third World. At the same time, with utmost cynicism the ideologists and propagandists of the system also maintain that such transfers mean "modernization" on the American model, as a result of which in due course people everywhere will be rich and happy in a fully automobilized society.

The much needed revolution means a fundamental change to all that. Nothing can be solved by overthrow alone. The overthrow or abolition of some institutions in specific historical situations is a necessary first step. Radical political acts are necessary in order to remove one type of personnel and to make it possible for something else to arise in its place. But the aim must be a profound process of ongoing social transformation. And in that sense the concept of revolution remains absolutely fundamental.

**N: Western workers, having organized unions, try to adjust their idea of Marx to the work situation in today's world. Their voice and struggle do not go beyond limited actions for welfare, higher wages, etc. In the East, on the other hand, because of dictatorship, delayed economic pressures and lack of theoretical knowledge the social movements aim not only at a better life, but also at the overthrow of their capital system. Globalization and privatization have created opportunities for movements against capitalism. The radical movement seems to originate from the East rather than the West. What do you think?**

**IM:** I think we have to examine the facts, and then you will find that some of what you say is right, but with historical qualifications. That is to say, what you describe reflects conditions of perhaps two or three decades ago, and less and less those of today. When you consider some crucial demands of the labor movement in Western capitalist countries, like France and Italy, they cannot be described as simply demands for improving wages. Take, for example, the demand for the 35 hours week without loss of pay, which has been granted by the French government. There is now in France a law—to be implemented in 2000-01—according to which the working week will be reduced to 35 hours. This is not a wage demand. The same thing is happening in Italy, where there is a very important push for the realization of the same objective. I can perhaps find a quotation for you from one of the leading figures in the Italian movement for the 35 hours week, Fausto Bertinotti. He had to answer a question coming from a woman reader of the daily paper of *Rifondazione*. As you know, the condition of women workers in all capitalist societies is worse than that of men. (Not that it is rosy by any means for their male counterparts.) She was asking the question: "If we have more hours for ourselves," as a result of the 35 hours working week, "how shall we utilize them?" This was Bertinotti's answer:

> When we say that it is not only a matter of trade union objectives, but of civilization, we are referring precisely to the horizon of the question you are posing: the important question of time, and the relationship between work-time and life-time. First of all, we know, from Marx, that the theft of work-time, at a certain stage of historical development, becomes a very miserable foundation of production and wealth and organization of society: moreover we know that the struggle against exploitation can only go together, be intertwined and closely connected with, the struggle against alienation; that is to say, against that mechanism deeply inherent in the nature of capitalism, which not only takes away from each worker the product of 'living labor', but induces estrangement, heterodirection and the oppressive regulation of lifetime. In this sense, the 35 hours, beyond the benefits they will be able to trigger off from the point of view of employment, do come back to the central question of the betterment of one's own life: of the self-government of time, to put it in non-contingent

political terms. Because there will not be a real social transformation without a project of collective self-government of working time and lifetime: a real project, not a hypothesis elaborated from the outside of the social subject and of individual subjectivities. This too is a great challenge for politics and for our party.

Now that is where you can see that the fight for the 35-hour week is not simply a "trade union demand." It challenges the whole system of social metabolic reproduction, and therefore it would be most inaccurate to describe it as nothing more than a "trade union demand."

You are right that for a long time economistic demands constituted the horizon of the labor movement in the advanced capitalist countries. But this narrow orientation cannot be maintained any longer. This connects us with the question of the chances for socialism. The labor movement is now pushed in the direction that it has to raise the question of work-time and lifetime. The reduction of work-time is to a very limited extent only a wage demand. The workers do not want simply an improvement in wages. True, they say, "We do not want to lose what we already have." But the objective logic of the situation is that they are losing it anyway for other reasons. One of the important losses of the last thirty years of capitalist development is what I call "the downward equalization of the differential rate of exploitation." (This is discussed in section 7 of The Necessity of Social Control, 1971, on "The Intensification of the Rate of Exploitation"; see Beyond Capital, 890–2.) In Western capitalist countries the working classes for a long time could enjoy the benefits of the "differential rate of exploitation." Their conditions of existence, conditions of work, were immeasurably better than what you had in the "underdeveloped countries" of the so-called Third World. (This is a concept that I have always rejected as the self-serving propaganda of Western capitalism, because the Third World is an integral part of the one and only, profoundly interconnected, world.)

Now, however, we find deteriorating conditions everywhere. The "downward equalization" is evidenced also in the most advanced capitalist countries. Now workers have to face being threatened in their basic conditions of existence, because unemployment—often camouflaged as "flexible" casualization—is spreading everywhere. Fighting against unemployment cannot be considered simply a wage negotiation. The time has passed a long time ago when you could treat "marginal unemployment"—at the peak of Keynesian expansion—in those terms. Thus the working classes even in the most advanced capitalist countries have to face up to this challenge.

You are, of course, right that the conditions are incomparably worse in the East. But it is important to stress that the countries concerned are an integral part of the system of "total social capital" and the "totality of labor." Anything that happens in one part has an impact on the conditions somewhere else. The conditions of the labor market are deteriorating everywhere, including the Western capitalist countries. This is true in Canada as much as in the United States, or in England, Germany, France and Italy. The pressures are intensifying and, I may add, this means a necessary change in the orientation of the Western working class movement. If you examine the history of the working class movement in the twentieth century, you will find that one of the great tragedies of this history was the internal division described as the separation of the so-called industrial arm of the movement (the trade unions) from the political arm (the political parties). This separation has meant the severe constraining of the labor movement, through confining its action to very narrow limits. The political parties are confined to a situation whereby the people they are supposed to represent have the chance to vote—to put a piece of paper into the ballot box once in every four or five years—and thereby renounce their power of decision making in favor of whoever is in parliament.

Now what is significant about the ongoing changes is that it becomes necessary to make the trade union movement itself (the "industrial arm") become directly political. This is now beginning to happen in some European capitalist countries (notably in France and Italy) as well as in Japan. And I trust that it will happen in the not too distant future also in Canada and in the United States. This is the qualification I would add to your question. Things have been and are significantly changing under the impact of the tendential law of capital's development for the downward equalization of the differential rate of exploitation in the age of the *structural crisis* of the *capital system as such*, and not simply of *capitalism*. You know what I am talking about; I discuss this problem in great detail in *Beyond Capital*. Under these conditions it is no longer possible for people to be kept in submission.

I can mention to you the British miners who waged a year-long struggle; not for wage improvement alone. It would be inconceivable to endure for a whole year the hardship, the misery, the discrimination, the hostility and the repression of the state for the sake of improving their wages by ten, twenty, or even fifty dollars per week, when they were losing much more even in financial terms in the course of their struggle. The miners in Britain were eventually defeated through the concerted action of the state and, sadly, as mentioned already, also of the Labour Party, their presumed "political arm." And what happened to the labor force of the British miners? At the time of the strike their numbers were in the region of 150,000; today this number is down to less than 10,000! This is the reality of the situation. This is what the workers had to fight against: the extermination of their numbers, the transformation of their mining towns and villages into the wasteland of unemployment. Thus, now more and more groups of workers also in the advanced capitalist countries are forced to proceed in the same way as the British miners did. I can also mention to you another case, the Liverpool dockworkers, who endured the extreme hardship of strike not for one year but for two and a half. This kind of action, this kind of struggle that is simultaneously industrial and political, is quite unthinkable within the narrow framework of "trade union objectives."

**N: Thank you for accepting our interview. Would you like to add anything for the Persian reader?**

**IM:** I can only wish great success to you all in our joint enterprise and struggle for a radical social transformation that we all badly need. And I trust that you will be moving in that way.

# NOTES

1. *The Power of Ideology* (New York: NYU Press), 1989, 462-470.
2. "Marxism Today," an interview published in *Radical Philosophy*, no. 62 (Autumn 1992), reprinted in Part IV of *Beyond Capital* (London: Merlin Press, 1995; distributed in the US by Monthly Review Press); quotation from *Beyond Capital*, 995-6.
3. Marx, *Grundrisse* (New York: Vintage, 1973), 488.
4. The argument that capital must be understood as a "mode of social metabolic control" rather than a static object is developed in detail in *Beyond Capital*, chapter 2.
5. Marx, *Grundrisse*, 408 and 410.
6. Ibid., 540.
7. Walt Rostow, *The Stages of Economic Growth* (Cambridge: Cambridge University Press, 1960), 155.
8. See a prominent editorial article in the London *Economist* entitled, "Time to bury Keynes?," (July 3, 1993, 21-22); a question answered by the Editors of *The Economist* with an emphatic "yes."
9. *The Economist*, December 31, 1991, 12.
10. A striking example of the differential rate of exploitation was given in an essay by a major Filipino historian and political thinker, Renato Constantino: "Ford Philippines, Inc., established only in 1967, is now [four years later] 37th in the roster of 1,000 biggest corporations in the Philippines. In 1971 it reported a return on equity of 121.32 percent, whereas its overall return on equity in 133 countries in the same year was only 11.8 percent. Aside from all the incentives extracted from the government, Ford's high profits were mainly due to cheap labor. While the US hourly rate for skilled labor in 1971 was almost $7.50, the rate for similar work in the Philippines was only $0.30." (Renato Constantino, *Neo-Colonial Identity and Counter-Consciousness: Essays in Cultural De-colonization* [London: Merlin Press, 1978], 234.) The relative privileges en-

joyed in the past by the working classes in the advanced capitalist countries have started to erode in the last three decades, as a result of capital's narrowing margins and of its ongoing transnational globalization. This downward equalization of the differential rate of exploitation is a most significant trend of development in our time, and it is bound to assert itself with increasing severity in the coming decades.

11. Rosa Luxemburg was prophetic in emphasizing the growing importance of militarist production, way back in 1913, pointing out that "Capital itself ultimately controls this automatic and rhythmic movement of militarist production through the legislature and a press whose function is to mold so-called 'public opinion.' That is why this particular province of capitalist accumulation at first seems capable of infinite expansion." (Rosa Luxemburg, *The Accumulation of Capital* [London: Routledge, 1963], 466.) The role of Nazi Fascism in further extending militarist production is obvious enough, as indeed is the prodigious (and quite prodigal) "extraneous help" provided to capital in "Western democracies" and elsewhere by the military industrial complex after the Second World War. An equally important, even if a somewhat different, kind of extraneous help was supplied to capital by all varieties of Keynesianism in the postwar decades. What is less obvious in this respect is the conscious dedication of F. D. Roosevelt to the same objective already before his election to the presidency. He even anticipated a condemnation of what later became known as "neo-liberalism," insisting—in a speech made on July 2, 1932—that "we should repeal immediately those provisions of law that compel the Federal Government to go into the market to purchase, to sell, to speculate in farm products in a futile attempt to reduce farm surpluses. And they are the people who are talking of *keeping Government out of business*" (F. D. Roosevelt, the New Deal Speech Before the Democratic Convention, Chicago, Illinois, 2 July 1932; all quotations from Roosevelt's speeches are taken from B.D. Zevin, ed., *Nothing to Fear: The Selected Addresses of Franklin Delano Roosevelt, 1932–1945* (London: Hodder & Stoughton, 1947).

12. Paul Baran, *The Political Economy of Growth* (New York: Monthly Review Press, 1957), vii.

13. *The Economist,* November 17, 1957.

14. The *Observer*'s comment on Roosevelt's First Inaugural Address, delivered in Washington D.C., March 4, 1933, quoted in Zevin, *Nothing to Fear*, 13.

15. F.D. Roosevelt, First Inaugural Address, March 4, 1933.

16. F.D. Roosevelt, Annual Message to Congress, Washington D.C., January 11, 1944.

17. P. C. No. 992, 23 February 1945. Quoted in Thomas H. Greer, *What Roosevelt Thought: The Social and Political Ideas of Franklin D. Roosevelt* (London: Angus & Robertson, 1958), 169.

18. Ibid.

19. F.D. Roosevelt, "Address on the Fiftieth Anniversary of the Statue of Liberty," New York City, October 28, 1936.

20. Harry Magdoff, *The Age of Imperialism: The Economics of US Foreign Policy* (New York: Monthly Review Press, 1966), 15.

21. Roosevelt did not try to hide that he wanted to justify his actions in the name of a warlike emergency. As he put it: "I shall ask the Congress for broad executive power to wage a war against the emergency, as great as the power that would be given to me if we were in fact invaded by a foreign foe." F. D. Roosevelt, First Inaugural Address.

22. F.D. Roosevelt, Second Inaugural Address, Washington D.C., January 20, 1937. Roosevelt also argued, in the same spirit, that little of the generated profit was "devoted to the reduction of prices. The *consumer was forgotten*. Very little of it went into increased wages: *the worker was forgotten*, and by no means an adequate proportion was even paid out in dividends—*the stockholder was forgotten*" (Roosevelt's "New Deal Speech"). The question *why* they were forgotten was not asked. The only thing that mattered was that now they are *remembered*, and therefore everything can and will be put right. What is missing from such discourse is the acknowledgement of overwhelming objective *incompatibilities*. This is what makes the Rooseveltian discourse on numerous occasions unrealistically rhetorical.

23. Daniel B. Schirmer, *Republic or Empire: American Resistance to the Philippine War* (Rochester, Vermont: Schenkman Books, n. d.), 1–3. The author also makes it clear, faithful to its original historical context, why the anti-imperialist movement at the turn of the century had to fail: "In 1902 George S. Boutwell, the chairman of the anti-imperialist league and erstwhile associate of Lincoln, concluded that the leadership of a successful struggle against imperialism was to lie in the hands of labor. He told a Boston audience of trade unionists: 'The final effort for the salvation of the republic is to be made by the laboring and producing classes.' If this was to be the case, it was obvious that American labor, at the moment, was not ready to shoulder its responsibility, dominated as it was by men like Gompers, who were unfolding a policy of conciliation with the trusts and support for their foreign policy. Whatever the future would hold for Boutwell's belief, at the time he spoke the anti-imperialists were declining in influence; they represented an ideology without a stable and growing social base" (ibid., 258).

24. The issue was not confined to French Indochina. Roosevelt's attitude was equally dismissive of would-be French aspirations for retaining possession of their North African colonies, notably Morocco. See in this respect his letter to Cordell Hull, dated January 24, 1944, quoted on p. 168 of T. H. Greer's book referred to in note 17 above.

25. See US Democratic Senator Daniel Patrick Moynihan's notorious book, *Pandaemonium: Ethnicity in International Relations* (New York: Oxford University Press, 1993).

26. Noam Chomsky, "The Current Bombings," *Spectre,* no. 7 (Summer 1999), 18.

27. Jeffrey Sachs, "Helping the World's Poorest," *The Economist,* August 14, 1999, 16 and 22.

28. Characteristically the *Economist*, in its editorial article on poverty in the "underdeveloped world," lays the stress on municipal matters ("reliable water supplies"—to be obtained through "water sellers," rather than "by struggling to install expensive piped supplies to the home"—and "safe drains" and "regular rubbish collections"), concluding that "The *main answers* lie in making *local government* more efficient and more accountable" ("Helping the Poorest," *The Economist,* August 14, 1999, 11). The truth is, of course, that the local governments of the countries in question are hopelessly handicapped by the resources made available to them by their national governments, which in their turn are most iniquitously locked into the self-perpetuating structural hierarchies of the global capital system.

29. Michael Heseltine's ministerial resignation statement, January 9, 1986, quoted in I. Mészáros, "The Present Crisis" (1987), reprinted in part IV of *Beyond Capital,* 952–964.

30. Ibid., 952.

31. Ibid., 954–958.

32. The good intentions of Jeffrey Sachs are clear when he writes, "the global regime on intellectual property rights requires a new look. The United States prevailed upon the world to toughen patent codes and cut down on intellectual piracy. But now transnational corporations and rich-country institutions are patenting everything from the human genome to rainforest biodiversity. The poor will be ripped off unless some *sense and equity* are introduced into this runaway process" (J. Sachs, op. cit., 22). However, he becomes hopelessly unrealistic where he describes the determinations behind the criticized policies as *"amazingly misguided"* (ibid., 16). There is nothing misguided about such policies, let alone "amazingly misguided," which suggests that they can be remedied by a good dose of rational illumination (like Roosevelt's "remembering" of those who had been "forgotten"). On the contrary, they are embodiments of callously deliberate, well calculated, and ruthlessly imposed decisions, emanating from capital's structurally safeguarded hierarchies and objective imperatives. The real issue is not the absence of the—now happily supplied—rational insight but the reality of overpowering *incompatibilities:* in Sachs' case that between "sense and equity." For what "sense" would recommend, the radical exclusion of all possible considerations of "equity" must absolutely deny. This is why Sachs' article—given the author's reverent attitude to "market society" (which cannot be even called by its proper name)—ends up with a totally fictitious "market solution."

33. Renato Constantino, *Identity and Consciousness: The Philippine Experience* (Quezon City: Malaya Books, 1974), 6. The Americans relinquished direct control of the Filipino educational system only in 1935, by which time they were exercising a very effective control over it indirectly.

34. On the disastrous US involvement in Vietnam, see Gabriel Kolko's seminal book, *Vietnam: Anatomy of a War, 1940–1975* (London: Allen & Unwin, 1986).

35. Andreas Papandreou told me in 1973 how he was released from the colonels' jail. A former member of President Kennedy's Brains Trust, John Kenneth

Galbraith, to his honor, went to see President Lyndon Johnson and pleaded with him on behalf of his old Harvard University friend. Johnson called in his secretary and asked her to connect him with the US ambassador in Athens. It was done on the spot and Johnson said to the Ambassador: 'Tell those sons of a bitch to release this good man, Papandreou, immediately'—which they did. For they knew very well who was really in charge in Greece. A few weeks before the overthrow of Mobutu's regime, the *Economist* quoted a US State Department official: "We know that he is a son of a bitch, but he is *our* son of a bitch." This description of a convenient ally dates back to Roosevelt's time, although it is a matter of some dispute whether Roosevelt himself or Cordell Hull used the term of Somoza.

36. István Mészáros, "Radical Politics and Transition to Socialism: Reflections on Marx's Centenary," first published in the Brazilian periodical *Escrita Ensaio*, Anno V, no. 11-12 (Summer 1983), 105–124. A shorter version of this article was delivered as a lecture in Athens in April 1983. The article is reprinted in full in Part IV of *Beyond Capital*, 937–951. The quotation is from 943–944 of the latter.

37. Shoji Niihara, "Struggle Against US Military Bases," *Dateline Tokyo*, No. 73, July 1999, 2.

38. József Ambrus, "A polgári védelem feladatai" (The Tasks of Civil Defense), in a special issue of *Ezredforduló*, dedicated to the problems of Hungary's entry into NATO, *Strategic Enquiries of the Hungarian Academy of Sciences* (1999), 32.

39. For a notable exception see John Manning's letter to *Spectre*, no. 6 (Spring 1999), 37–38. On a related issue see *US Military Bases in Japan: A Japan-US Dialogue*, Report from the Boston Symposium, April 25, 1998, Cambridge, MA.

40. Tetsuzo Fuwa, "Address to Japan Peace Committee in Its 50th Year," *Japan Press Weekly*, July 3, 1999, 15. Comparing Japanese Prime Minister Obuchi to leading opposition figure Fuwa the *Economist* grudgingly wrote: "Events so far tended to show Mr Obuchi as a bumbling amateur, especially when grilled by consummate professionals such as Tetsuzo Fuwa" ("A Pity about Uncle Obuchi," the *Economist*, November 20, 1999, 97–98.

41. This is already happening as Japan is compelled to pay for the massive cost of US military occupation through their numerous bases in the country. "Costs that the Japanese government bore in 1997 for maintaining US bases in Japan reached 4.9 billion US dollars, ranking first among other countries of the world (according to the Allied Contribution to the Common Defense, 1999 Report). For each US soldier stationed in Japan, this is 122,500 US dollars." (S. Niihara, op. cit., 3.)

42. *Akahata*, November 1, 1999; quoted in *Japan Press Weekly*, November 6, 1999, 6–7.

43. S. Niihara, op. cit., 3.

44. "Washington tells China to back off or risk Cold War," *The Daily Telegraph*, May 16, 1999, 15. The same article also tells us that "The spate of espionage stories seems to have been leaked by figures within the Republican Party or the Pentagon who see it in the long-term interests of the United States to have

one big enemy." Obviously, Saddam Hussein is not big enough to satisfy the ideological requirements and the increasing military expenditure corresponding to the long-term design of the aggressive US imperialist posture.

45. Jonathan Story, "Time Is Running Out for the Solution of the Chinese Puzzle," *Sunday Times,* July 1, 1999, 25.

46. Ibid. Jonathan Story's article is an extract from his book: *The Frontiers of Fortune* (London: Financial Times/Prentice Hall, 1999).

47. The importance of Turkey as a US "local assistant" has been dramatically exposed this spring with the ignominious consignment of Abdullah Ocalan, the leader of the Kurdish PKK, to Ankara, under great US pressure, humiliating the various European "local assistants" involved in this affair. See Luigi Vinci, *La socialdemocrazia e la sinistra antagonista in Europa* (Milan, Edizioni Punto Rosso, 1999), 13. See also Fausto Bertinotti, *Per una società alternativa: Intervista sulla politica, sul partito e sulle culture critiche,* interviewed by Giorgio Riolo (Milan: Edizioni Punto Rosso, 1999), 30–31.

48. The quotations in this paragraph are all from "The New Geopolitics," *The Economist,* July 31, 1999, 15–16.

49. David Watts, "Howard's 'Sheriff' role angers Asians," *The Times,* September 27, 1999, 14.

50. Ibid.

51. Ibid.

52. Jonathan Story, op. cit., 33.

53. See David Cay Johnston, "Gap Between Rich and Poor Found Substantially Wider," *New York Times*, September 5, 1999.

54. "Worried in Beijing," *The Economist,* August 7, 1999, 14.

55. Ibid. The necessary overthrow of China is several times eagerly prognosticated in this editorial article.

56. See a thought-provoking discussion of these problems in Luigi Vinci's volume quoted in note 47, in particular 60–66.

57. "Superpower Europe," *The Economist,* July 17, 1999, 14.

58. Rupert Cornwell, "Europe warned not to weaken NATO," *The Independent,* October 8, 1999, 18.

59. Ibid.

60. For an illuminating history of the American labor movement see Paul Buhle, *Taking Care of Business: Samuel Gompers, George Meany, Lane Kirkland, and the Tragedy of American Labor* (New York: Monthly Review Press, 1999), in particular 17–90 and 204–263. An insightful account of the strategic role of unionized labor today is by Michael D. Yates, *Why Unions Matter* (New York: Monthly Review Press, 1998).

61. To be sure, acknowledging the existence of unfavorable objective circumstances cannot provide a blanket justification for the often self-imposed contradictions of the "subjective side." Michael Yates rightly stresses the

historical impact and responsibility of the individuals who were in a position of making decisions as protagonists of the American labor movement. He writes in a recent article, "Gompers did not have to betray IWW and the militant socialist cadre to the police, but then again leading socialists did not have to ally themselves with Gompers and eventually become as rabidly conservative as he. Gompers and his progeny did not have to commit themselves to US imperialism and undermine progressive workers' movements throughout the world, taking money from the CIA even as this agency of death was encouraging the murder and imprisonment of union leaders around the globe. CIO leaders did not have to join in the witch-hunts, making the CIO virtually indistinguishable from the AFL by the time of their merger in 1955. But neither did the communists have to urge the government to lock up the Trotskyists and slavishly follow the directives of Stalin. All of this is not to say that the actions of some radicals and those of Gompers, et al., are on the same plane, but to say that radicals made their own history, too." Michael D. Yates, "The Road Not Taken," *Monthly Review* 51:6 (November 1999), 40.

62. Denis Noble, "Academic Integrity," in Alan Montefiore and David Vines, eds., *Integrity in the Public and Private Domains* (London & New York: Routledge, 1999), 184.

63. Otto Nathan and Heinz Norden, eds., *Einstein on Peace* (New York: Schocken Books, 1960), 343. Einstein's message could only be published posthumously.

64. Ibid., p. 107.

65. Ibid., p. 116.

66. Ibid., p. 344.

67. Quoted in Ronald W. Clark, *Einstein: The Life and Times* (London: Hodder & Stoughton, 1973), 552.

68. Marx, *The Poverty of Philosophy,* in Marx and Engels, *Collected Works,* vol. 6 (New York: International Publishers, 1976), 210.

69. Ibid., 212.

70. See chapter 18 of *Beyond Capital,* 673–738. An earlier version of this chapter was contained in the study entitled: "Il rinnovamento del marxismo e l'attualità storica dell'offensiva socialista," published in *Problemi del socialismo* (a journal founded by Lelio Basso), Anno XXIII (January-April 1982), 5–141.

71. We should not forget that anti-labor legislation in Britain started under Harold Wilson's Labour government, with the legislative venture called "In place of strife," at the initial phase of capital's structural crisis. It continued under Edward Heath's short-lived government, and then again under Wilson's and Callaghan's Labour governments. Ten years later, under Margaret Thatcher, it received an openly "neo-liberal" stamp.

72. Luigi Vinci, *La socialdemocrazia e la sinistra antagonista in Europa* (Milan: Edizioni Punto Rosso, 1999), 69.

# INDEX